JAPAN DIARY
of cross-cultural mission

Also by J. Lawrence Driskill:

Mission Adventures in Many Lands

JAPAN DIARY
of cross-cultural mission

by
j. lawrence driskill

assisted by
lillian cassel driskill

Hope Publishing House

Pasadena, California

1993

Distributed by Spring Arbor Distributors

For information address:
Hope Publishing House
Southern California Ecumenical Council
P. O. Box 60008
Pasadena, California 91116 - U.S.A.
Telephone (818) 792-6123; FAX (818) 792-2121

Cover design - Michael McClary/The Workshop

 - Printed in the U.S.A. on acid-free, recycled paper.

Library of Congress Cataloging-in-Publication Data

Driskill, J. Lawrence, 1920-
        Japan diary of cross-cultural mission / by J. Lawrence Driskill :
assisted by Lillian Cassel Driskill ; with a foreword by J. Dudley
Woodberry.
              p.   cm.
        Includes index.
        ISBN 0-932727-63-8 : $17.95. -- ISBN 0-932727-62-X (pbk.) : $11.95
        1. Driskill, J. Lawrence, 1920-   --Diaries.   2. Missionaries--
Japan--Diaries. 3. Missionaries--United States--Diaries.
I. Driskill, Lillian Cassel. II. Title.
BV3457.D75A3 1993
266'.009'2--dc20   92-43636
        [B]   CIP

Dedicated to our parents

Roy and Ethel Cassel
and
Elijah (Hut) and Annie Driskill

With many thanks to all
who helped make this book possible.

Contents

Foreword

This is a day when many people are only committing themselves to short-term missions or are studying the theory of missions before they have much or any experience. Larry Driskill's Diary provides a valuable resource for such people by adding the flesh of experience to the bones of theory, for it describes the life and consequent lessons of a couple who committed themselves to the long haul of living for Christ as members of another culture.

Like the facets of a diamond the vignettes throw light, not only on life in Japan, but on what is involved in adjusting to any culture. The stories reveal religious yearnings, how festivals express these feelings, and how political and national aspirations can develop into anti-Christian as well as anti-Western sentiments. At times the reader is amused by the awkward situations that can arise through customs such as communal baths, and at other times, humbled by how much there is to learn from non-Christians in areas such as love for God's creation.

Other accounts give psychological insights into, for example, the philosophy of childrearing and the role of such institutions as theater in providing emotional release for the rigid mores that hold society together. Throughout, the reader sees how a wholistic concern for the range of felt needs of people of another culture provides opportunities for interpreting our faith. As with the diamond, the facets reflect light and enjoyment.

—Dr. J. Dudley Woodberry, Dean
School of World Mission, Fuller Theological Seminary

Introduction/Acknowledgments

For missionaries to share the good news of God's love and forgiveness in Christ with people of another culture, several things are necessary. They need an understanding of the Bible and basic Christian theology combined with a keen sense of the language and culture of the people they seek to serve.

It is difficult to communicate the gospel, or even friendly intentions, if one does not know how these will be perceived by the listener. By making the effort and taking the time to become immersed in new morés and a strange language, career missionaries communicate to the local people that they love and care for them enough to put forth the effort to learn the language and adapt to their culture.

In the following "diary" I try to illustrate the problems we faced as new missionaries in Japan and how we struggled to learn the language and culture so we could win people to Jesus Christ. My wife and I finally realized that our "tired" feeling was caused by the strain and stress of learning a new language and culture, in addition to the busy work load of missionary preaching, teaching and sharing people's burdens.

Chronicled here are the spiritual, physical, mental and psychological problems we faced in the first years on the mission field. I wish we could have read a report like this before going to Japan, for it surely would have helped us to become more sensitive and effective missionaries. Although cultures differ, the problems remain similar for every missionary.

I am grateful to all those who helped to make this book possible, especially to Ms. Faith Annette Sand, who worked long and hard to get this book edited and published and to Sharon Sand for her faithful and effective work in putting this manuscript into computer-eze.

"... go and make disciples of all nations ..."
—Matthew 28:19 (NIV)

Prologue

The beginning did not seem auspicious. We were so frightened all we wanted to do was to get back home as quickly as possible. The scare we had on the day we moved into our new home to begin our first missionary assignment in Japan left us badly shaken. Only help from God and our Japanese Christian friends prevented us from returning home to America after the shock of that day. Our missionary career almost ended on the day it was to begin.

We were moving from language school study in the beautiful city of Kyoto with its colorful temples and shrines to the natural beauty of the rural town of Nagano-cho—which is about 30 miles south of the big industrial metropolis of Osaka, Japan's second largest city. At five A.M. we were up getting ready for the moving truck which was expected at seven A.M. The hour came and went but the truck was nowhere in sight. Finally a Japanese friend, Mori-san, telephoned the movers who dwadles in at nine A.M. After loading up, the truck driver asked me to ride with him to show the way to our new home, some 70 miles away.

Lillian, my wife, went by train carrying nine-month old Edward in her arms. Ayako-san, a young woman who had been helping in our home while we studied the language, went along to help carry the bags Lillian needed to take care of Edward. They had difficulty getting a taxi and so missed the train they planned to go on. Beyond this, the train workers were on strike so only a few trains were running and it ended up they had to ride four different trains in order to reach Nagano-cho.

Ayako-san had to return immediately to Kyoto to take care of her own home duties, so Lillian was met at the station by Pastor Hashimoto, who helped take her bags across the narrow bridge over Ishikawa River to the Japanese-style apartment we were renting. New friends from the local church were waiting at the apartment to help her get settled in. They had already put up a bed in an upstairs room where she and the baby could rest.

It was a hot July day and there was no air conditioning, so Lillian took off all of the baby's clothing, including his diaper, to give him some relief from the sticky heat. She put him on the bed and with that lightening speed babies can generate, he suddenly crawled over to a window beside the bed and started to pull himself up against this second floor window. As he did so the French-style windows swung outward and he started to fall through.

Lillian lunged to grab him but since he had no clothes on, there was nothing to hold onto and his little foot slipped right through her hand. Down he went, kicking and screaming, in a long fall to the ground. Being new in the house, Lillian didn't know where he had fallen to or even what dangers lurked below. As everyone does in a straw-mat Japanese home, she had taken off her shoes, so she dashed down the stairs barefoot and ran out the door screaming, "Help! Help!" in English for in her panic she had completely forgotten all her Japanese. She turned the corner of the apartment house in time to see a young man picking up the baby who was bleeding from cuts and bruises all over his body. Another friend ran to get Dr. Sawada who soon arrived to do whatever he could for the baby's wounds.

When I arrived with the furniture truck Lillian was in an almost total state of shock but she managed to say, "I think I've killed our son." The baby was covered with small white bandages and was either in a coma or asleep, I couldn't tell which. For the rest of the day Lillian sat without speaking, moving back and forth in a rocking chair while our church friends helped us unpack.

When they had gone and the time came to get dinner I asked Lillian, "What shall we do for dinner?" Her response was to look at me blankly and say, "Dinner?" as if she couldn't remember what the word meant. I was in something of a state of shock myself, worrying about the baby and about her. However, with the assistance of the high school girl who had come to be our new helper I managed to cook some eggs and make a tomato salad. Not a very fancy dinner to celebrate our first day in the new home.

It was a rough night but by the next day both the baby and Lillian were much better. We discovered that what saved Edward in his 15-foot fall onto a bed of rocks was that he fell through a willow tree whose branches slowed him down. Tadayoshi, the landlord's son, saw him fall and said he was grabbing at every branch with a clear instinct to survive.

"I wonder if this means we should give up our mission work and go back home? Or was this just a time of testing?" asked Lillian after the shock had worn off. I didn't tell her that when I first saw them after the accident, I had feared that even life and sanity were hanging in the balance, including my own.

But God helped us to stay in Japan and we felt God's blessing and help throughout our time there, not only as the leaders in starting three new churches—in Kaizuka, Misasagi and Senri-Newtown—but also in helping the development of six other new churches, in assisting the Seikyo Gakuen Christian School expand from a beginning class of 40 students to its present size of over 2,000 today.

We had to face many other shocks and troubles in Japan, but God, and our Japanese Christian friends, helped us get through all of them. In the following pages we share with you the story of those challenging missionary adventures we had in Japan.

I

First Steps with a New Language and Culture

Feb. 19, 1951—Yokohama

Arriving in Japan's chief harbor in darkness we found ourselves in the midst of a ghostly forest of ship masts piercing the sky around us like tall, naked trees—an immediate reminder that Japan is a maritime nation, a successful trader and the world's foremost shipbuilder.

By God's grace we had arrived in Japan after preparing for it since being appointed by our Board of Foreign Missions in May 1949. Our journey on to Tokyo brought many new impressions. We began to try out our newly acquired language skills on the shop and road signs we passed—and could recognize the signs for bookstore, bakery and food market, but difficult road signs reminded us that we still had a lot of language study ahead. We could not find our way around or effectively communicate God's love to anyone until we had become more proficient in Japanese—perhaps the most difficult language in the world.

Along the streets we passed many small houses, partly hidden by walls and hedges. In this crowded country many have learned to protect their privacy. Some people are dressed in kimonos, others in Western dress. Surprisingly, the people appear more cheerful and healthier looking than we had expected so soon after the debacle of World War II.

Looking at their calm faces it is hard to believe they were such fierce fighters in the war; or that countless thousands of them died a martyr's death here in the days of Francis Xavier.

Over 30,000 were massacred in the Shimabara Rebellion of 1638 led by five oppressed Christian Samurai, according to historian G.B. Sansom. Others who refused to deny Christ were thrown over cliffs, tied to a stake on the seashore to slowly drown in the incoming tide or sawed in two.

Feb. 20, 1951—Tokyo

Our friends who met us at the ship—the Hannafords and Kamitsukas—took us to the Oltmans' home in Tokyo to spend the night. This morning I was awakened by an unusual clacking noise. Looking out the window I found that it was made by wooden clogs (*geta*) clacking on the street as people hurried by on their way to work or to school.

The Oltmans are gracious hosts and Lillian and our four-month old son, Edward, seem to be adjusting well to the new situation. In a few days we will go on to Kyoto but first we must get our baggage through customs and sent on its way. I hope that running out of gas on our way into Tokyo yesterday is not a portent of difficulties in getting ourselves and our baggage to Kyoto.

It was intimidating but I managed to go to Yokohama alone today and check trunks through customs and buy tickets for Kyoto. Paul Oltman was supposed to go with me to help, but something came up and he couldn't go. His trust in my language ability to get things through customs was a vote of confidence I appreciated. I made a deposit of ¥2,000 (some $6) with Nippon Express and the rest is to be paid when the baggage is delivered in Kyoto.

Feb. 21, 1951

We have now been shown a good part of Tokyo by the Oltmans and Hannafords who drove us around. The sights which impressed us were the palace grounds with their tremendous walls and moats; modern brick, stone and concrete buildings; well-stocked fruit and vegetable markets; department stores filled with a vast array of inventory; three-wheeled Japanese pickup trucks and thousands of bicycles of every shape and size.

There are hordes of people everywhere, especially on trains and streetcars. To travel at rush hour is to risk one's life in the shoving, heaving crowd replete with official "pushers" to help thrust people in so the train doors can close.

Feb. 22, 1951

We were up early to finish packing and get to the station to leave for Kyoto. The military train proved quite comfortable (luxurious for post-war Japan). In the diner we were served an American-style dinner with good beef for 40¢ military script. Along the way we saw fitting tributes to God's creative work in Japan—lofty mountains, enchanting sea inlets, quaint villages nestled in mountain valleys. We were never out of sight of houses or people. This is a new and thrilling experience.

Lillian found it embarrassing to nurse our baby son in the same car with soldiers, but their generous provision of this comfortable transportation brought us to our own duty stations—a bit different from theirs. There is some war damage around us but we are pleasantly surprised at how well Japan has recovered in such a short time.

We were met in Kyoto by Newton Thurber, the Glen Johnsons, Virginia Deter, Dot Taylor, Gwyllum Lloyd, Malcom Carrick and even Pearl and Dick Drummond from Kobe. What a privilege to have such splendid coworkers to encourage us in this new field of service for Christ's Kingdom.

Feb. 23, 1951—Kyoto

We are staying with the Thurbers until we can rent our own apartment. This afternoon we went to see an apartment offered by Dr. and Mrs. Mori who rent out the upstairs part of their home while they and their little daughter live downstairs.

For this first visit in a Japanese home we took off our shoes at the entrance, bowed and were ushered into the living room to sit on the floor around a low table. Both of our hosts were dressed in Japanese kimonos. We made small talk until the wife had prepared tea and after leisurely drinking this, we began to get down to business. They showed us the upstairs apartment which has three large rooms, a kitchen and toilet facilities and abundant storage space built into the walls. We agreed to pay ¥9,000 (almost $30) a month for rent plus ¥1,000 ($3) for utilities.

The maid who had served the previous tenants agreed to stay on to help us with shopping, cleaning, baby care and household chores which will help free us to learn as much language as possible in the six months allotted us in the local Japanese language school. Her name is Ayako-san and we found out that she was just married four months ago. She will be a big help.

On the way to see this apartment I got an interesting lesson in Japanese food etiquette. One cannot eat food in public, such as we might do with an ice cream or candy bar. Newton and I had been observing classes at the language school until about two P.M. but I had had no opportunity to eat the sandwich I had along for lunch. The problem was solved by finding a small deserted courtyard in a nearby temple where I could eat without offending passersby.

March 4, 1951

At long last we are settled in a "Temporary Home." Our furniture may take months getting here so we are getting along the best we can with the minimum of a bed, a table and chairs and kitchen utensils borrowed from friends.

Our worst problem is the lack of heat. The only room with a heater is the living room. We were trying to sleep in our bedroom with two sheets and two blankets on twin beds shoved together, but last night we moved into the dining room which has an upper and lower bunk built into the wall. We finally ended up sleeping on the narrow bottom bunk, huddled together for warmth. Fortunately spring is not too far off and next winter we should have our own heaters with us.

Ayako-san comes in almost every day and is indispensable as we are busy studying the language. She gets paid the going rate of ¥1,000 a week, but she is worth a fortune. We will try to show our gratitude with extra gifts from time to time. She eats lunch with us and is quite helpful with the language problems we face, such as applying for the necessary rice ration, (a leftover from the war economy).

The landlady, Mrs. Mori, came up today to get some Japanese bedding *(futon)* stored in our closets. She joked that if her husband was an American he would be doing this for her, but a Japanese husband would never do such a thing! I laughed and was proud that I understood her.

The most frustrating thing about living here is not being able to comprehend what is being said. Lillian says she feels almost "illiterate" not being able to make a telephone call or exchange pleasantries with a neighbor. Even though I have had a bit more language study than she, I still feel the same frustration. Hopefully in six months we will improve enough for independent living and be able to share the good news of God's love in simple terms.

March 9, 1951

We had quite a celebration for Lillian's birthday today. Since Dot Taylor's birthday is on the 13th, Ginny Deter invited us all to her home for a joint celebration. When I went to the flower shop for a corsage I had to show the girl there how to make it. Apparently corsages are not a common custom in this part of Japan.

The Japanese money we carry is huge. Paper bills are about four by six inches in size and Lillian calls them "large sheets of paper." For a present I gave her a large wallet to carry these in. We also had a small private celebration at home with a pretty cake I found in a bakery.

We have bought or borrowed enough dishes, pots and pans, linens, and furniture to get along until our things arrive by freighters. Edward who is now five months old is adjusting well to life in Japan. Among all the black-haired children he is a great novelty with his light blonde hair and the Japanese children love to touch his hair.

March 18, 1951

Yesterday Lillian and I took a holiday from studies to tour the fascinating palace grounds here. We entered just in time to join a group of school children on their tour and ended up having a great time of fellowship and fun with them. Kyoto was the capital city of Japan for over a thousand years and the palace buildings are a national treasure with huge polished timbers for floors, beams and ceilings, with decorated sliding doors and straw mats (*tatami*) covering huge rooms.

We were shown a tree just outside the emperor's bedroom and told it was his "alarm clock" because the birds singing there awakened him each morning. The garden filled with exotic arrangements of stones, fish ponds, shrubs and flowers is magnificent.

Afterward we lunched at the O.S.S. store (Overseas Service Store) of which we have three in Kyoto and then went to see a Japanese movie, as it started to rain. There are American movies here, too. Life is not dull!

From some shops and homes come the sounds of Western songs such as "Chattanooga Choo Choo" but even with the obvious interest in Western goods, I wonder how much this will influence Japanese life on a deeper level. Are they really open to Christian concepts of God, Christ or even the Christian concept of family?

The church we visited this morning is losing its pastor and we would like to help out there but we shall wait to see how God leads us. It may be just what we have been praying for.

March 24, 1951—Easter Sunday

I attended the Easter Sunday Sunrise Service this morning, held in a large amphitheater near here with both Japanese and English being used. There was a good spirit of community worship transcending our racial and cultural differences. Lillian couldn't share in it or in the special English service held in the afternoon, as she had caught cold.

Of course we had to prepare for these big events with our usual soak in the Japanese bath called *ofuro*—which is a wooden tub just large enough for one person to sit in with legs bent. There is a wooden step leading down into it that covers the metal pipes which heat the water. It is necessary to fill the tub first which takes about 15-20 minutes, then turn on the gas and wait about two hours until the water is quite hot.

Mrs. Mori has been preparing this for me, but I felt guilty and asked Mr. Mori to show me how so I could do it. He said "I don't know how, my wife always does that."

She agreed to show me how. The first time we went down to the tub room, we put our heads down under the tub together to see where to light it. I couldn't help but wonder what her husband would think if he happened to walk in and find us almost "cheek-to-cheek."

There are wooden covers to keep the water hot as the whole family uses the same water. The idea is to wash off first by pouring water over your body with little wooden basins using the soap before you get into the tub to soak (no soap allowed there). Unfortunately the floor is very cold in the winter and it can be wretched pouring the water over yourself and watching it gurgle down the drain. When you are rinsed, it is miserable to get into the tub because it is too hot and you dare not cool it as the next person wants it hot.

Men and women bathe in the same large pool in public bathing houses. One American man went there and had quite a hectic time. Just as he got undressed a strange woman came in. To hide his embarrassment he jumped into the hot water too quickly and got burned which made him jump out again, in again, out again repeatedly. The Japanese people in the room were quite entertained. Japanese bath etiquette requires that people pretend not to see each other, in addition they discretely turn their backs and use wash cloths or small towels to cover critical spots. My experience in public baths is limited but I can affirm that they do manage to maintain their dignity.

April 1, 1951

Last Friday we attended our first meeting of the Kyodan (United Church related) missionary group here. After three afternoons spent in bed, Lillian is over her cold and this opportunity for fellowship with friends cheered her up. Our Swiss doctor is helpful.

Young Arlo Johnson has the measles and we hope Edward will not get them. At five-and-a half months Edward wakes up starved at five A.M. and Lillian has to nurse him even though she is half asleep.

Lillian is learning how to shop but overspent at the store the other day and was pleased when the store "charged" it until her next visit. Recently Mrs. Mori came rushing up and said the *nikuya* (butcher) was at the door, did we need meat? We learned a new custom—the butcher is closed on days that have a "6" in them (6, 16, 26) so on those days sells meat door-to-door. Most vegetables except celery and head lettuce can be bought in local markets. New to us are large Japanese persimmons, pears shaped like apples, loquats and great pyramids of colorful mandarin oranges in the markets. It is also a bit unusual to see white radishes almost two feet long and four inches in diameter. Fish is plentiful but beef is scarce and expensive. Chicken is common but usually not refrigerated so it is best to buy it on the "hoof" and have the butcher slaughter it while you wait.

April 8, 1951

It is now *hanami* (flower-viewing) time and everyone goes out to see the cherry blossoms. On the way home from church we went by the Heian Shrine (Shinto) to see the unusual "weeping willow" style cherry blossoms there. The shrine has a tremendous *Torii* (sacred gate) about 20 feet high and painted vermillion with large temples of the same color. Inside it is more subdued with straw mat floors and tastefully decorated sliding doors. The altar is crowded with somewhat gaudy utensils. An offering box with slots at the top stands conspicuously at the door. Large straw ropes hang down near it and the vermillion pillars are covered with folded paper prayers.

Occasionally an elderly lady comes up, pulls the rope to ring a bell which gets the attention of the god enshrined there, makes a fervent prayer and puts her offering in the box. Few men or young people seem to be interested in the prayers but they do flock to see the cherry blossoms. To enter the shrine or temple you must remove your shoes and walk around in stocking feet, even in the winter.

It is election time here and every day, all day, sound trucks are going around the neighborhood campaigning. The noise is disturbing but it is Japan's attempt at democracy. Political issues are barely touched upon, the emphasis being "please vote for our candidate."

Churches are beginning to react against American customs and are trying to become independent and free of foreign influence. Using the Japanese harp (koto) in worship is becoming popular in some churches and Japanese hymns are being sung. Democracy and Western ways have been imposed from the top down and it is natural for the Japanese to want to develop their own way of life and worship.

Democracy will probably survive but it will be a type of Japanese democracy, not American.

April 15, 1951

Last Saturday afternoon a local pastor came with the wife of a prosperous businessman asking if I would teach an English Bible class in the lady's home on Sunday evenings from 7 to 9 P.M. The Lord is opening the way for us to begin a witness. Even though many will come only to practice their English, it is still an opportunity to tell others about God's love in Christ Jesus. I agreed to do it. It is good to be able to continue language study and witness at the same time.

A few of my fellow students in the Japanese language school seem to think our studies are a waste of time. They would prefer to be "out there winning souls." I feel the best way to win souls is to show enough respect and love for the people to be willing to learn their language first. Besides this is necessary in order to share the good news of the gospel adequately and to be able to communicate with them. Before we can teach we must learn—their language and their needs.

Some non-Christians here seem to have a deeper love for God's created world of nature than I do. We need to learn why. What is their experience with God's "general revelation?" Special revelation in and through Christ will follow.

April 22, 1951

We are learning more about the Japanese people each day. For example, even though the emperor publicly renounced the idea that he is "divine," people still hold him in "reverence." The Shinto festival on May 15th (*Aoi Matsuri*) honors the emperor, including a "sacred carriage" in which the emperor used to ride. He has two palaces in Kyoto—Nijo Castle and the *Gosho* (honorable place) plus the magnificent castle in Tokyo.

People come from all over Japan to have the privilege of working in the palace grounds in Tokyo. There is a waiting list of over a thousand to clean up and do whatever is necessary there. I cannot imagine such enthusiasm for cleaning our White House and grounds! Women here even keep the streets in front of their homes swept clean. People seem to have a sense of responsibility toward their whole community. What contrast to our litter-bug habits in America! I hope the Japanese don't lose this good trait as they absorb some of the real blessings of American democracy.

I am pleased that I have been invited to preach at the Rakuhoku Church on May 20th. Before that, on the 13th, I speak at the English worship service.

April 29, 1951

Yesterday all three of us went to Nagano-cho in Osaka Prefecture to visit a church and school which has invited us to help there as cooperating missionaries. Our fellow missionary Louis Grier met us in Osaka and Toru Hashimoto, the pastor, met us at the Nagano-cho train station.

The pastor is 29 years old and energetic but seems to be greatly overworked. He has about ten Sunday school meetings in the area in addition to his main church and several preaching points in believers' homes. The school, Seikyo

Gakuen, has just begun this month with 40 students in a small building completed on a hill overlooking the downtown area of this small town of 17,000.

The school was started by a young public school teacher, Noboru Nakayama, assisted by an older teacher and former junior high principal, Shinichi Ueda. Both are elders in the local church and have a vision of training new leadership for Japan through this Christian junior high with plans to develop to the college level eventually. We would help with evangelistic work and the school.

This seems to be the most promising prospect for our field of service that has been presented so far. While still in the U.S. we had a letter from Rev. Gordon Chapman inviting us to serve in Asahigawa on the northern island of Hokkaido, but the powers that be in Tokyo didn't seem to like that idea.

Our mission representative, Howard Hannaford, recently wrote suggesting a part-time assignment in the city of Shimizu with half time spent in continued language study. Since we like the Nagano-cho possibility I immediately telephoned Mr. Hannaford requesting that it be seriously considered at the May 1st meeting where the decision will supposedly be made. I followed the call with a detailed telegram telling about Nagano-cho.

Tonight I begin the seven-to-nine P.M. Bible class in the home. I hope to change the time to Thursday as the young people in the church we attend want to have one on Sunday evenings. The schedule is becoming hectic already and Lillian has a touch of the flu. I hope Edward and I don't get it and that Lillian will be well soon.

May 7, 1951

The new Bible Class I am teaching went quite well last night. Although some of the students may come because of a chance to learn English it is obvious as we study God's Word that a hunger for spiritual food motivates most of them. Japanese people lost their national pride and spiritual foundation in Shinto when they lost the war. By God's grace we hope to fill the vacuum with the gospel of God's love for them.

Yesterday afternoon was spent with a young man we met on the train to Nagano-cho. He was dressed in a dark blue school uniform and had brown eyes that sparkled with interest. He asked to visit and came armed with a gift of a lovely girl doll in traditional kimono. He stayed so long we invited him to have supper with us and he accepted. At 6:30 P.M. I had to excuse myself to go teach the Bible Class or he might have stayed all evening. He is certainly eager to talk to us.

We are now officially appointed to work at Nagano-cho and will probably move there about July 12th. We are negotiating to rent an apartment built adjoining a relatively wealthy person's home. Originally it was meant to house the elderly parents of the wife, Mrs. Hayakawa, but they died before it was completed. There is a separate entrance but we would need to add a kitchen, as the wife's parents intended to eat with her and didn't need a kitchen. It is all straw mat floors except the bathroom which has a Western toilet seat with a modified septic tank, but no flush mechanism.

Everything is so uncertain with the Korean War still going on that our mission board is hesitant to build new homes, even though it was previously decided to build new ones to replace those lost in the bombing and fires of World War II. We are willing to live in this Japanese style apartment if that seems best.

Last Saturday, the fifth day of the fifth month, was a national holiday here called *Koi Nobori*. It is a children's festival and the custom is to fly large carp-shaped fish flags on high poles if there is one or more young sons in the family. The carp is a male symbol of strength and courage, as the carp swims upstream against the current. Now some of the male chauvinism has been taken out of the holiday for the name has been changed from "Boys' Day" to "Children's Day," and girls get a smaller red flag to fly under the boy's blue one.

Other special days include the Girl's Doll Festival on the third day of the third month when every home is supposed to display a set of 15 or more elaborately dressed dolls symbolizing members of the imperial court. Another is *Tanabata*, the Festival of the Weaver based on the legend of the weaving maid, the star Vega, who fell in love with and married the herdsman, the star Altair. Being too busy with love they neglected their duties and the weaver's father, the Ruler of Heaven, henceforth allowed them to meet only one day a year—the seventh day of the seventh month. The early custom was to emphasize the virtue of the domestic duties of women, but now it centers more on fun and romance. It is celebrated by decorating a small bamboo tree (or a large branch) with colorful strips of paper symbolizing love notes and poems.

A major religious holiday is *O-bon*, commemorated on July 13th in some places and the middle of August in others. It is believed that this is when the spirits of the dead return to their former homes. People illumine their way home by setting out beautifully decorated paper lanterns holding a candle (or bulb) inside. It was enchanting to see long lines of these lights displayed on boats floating down the river. This is also a time when you see genuine folk dancing with people in a circle, dancing, singing and clapping their hands rhythmically.

The New Year's celebration is the most popular of all—a three-day splurge of eating, drinking hot rice wine and visiting. This is the one time when people not normally active in any formal religious practice will visit temples and shrines their family has been traditionally related to, including a visit to the graves of close relatives. Interestingly, Christmas is becoming almost as popular as New Year's but the emphasis is on Santa Claus, Christmas "decoration cakes" and shopping rather than as the birthday of Jesus. Some say the popularity of Christmas has resulted in many Japanese taking the birthday of Buddha more seriously than they did in the past.

May 12, 1951
Went to Kobe today to check on our freight as we had been told that the freighter was due in today. However there was a strike in Kobe and the warehouses are closed on Saturday afternoon and Sunday, so we couldn't find out much.

However, the local Japan Express people assured us that they could take care of everything and would send our freight directly to Nagano-cho. There the pastor will store it under waterproof tarps in the church yard until we arrive in July.

While in Kobe we treated ourselves to a chocolate nut sundae at the Overseas Service Store (O.S.S.) since good ice cream is not yet available in Nagano-cho. We saw lots of rickshaws in Kobe but didn't get to ride in one. On the way home I had a long talk with some U.S. sailors who were on a sightseeing tour from "Stateside."

May 20, 1951

Preached twice today, at Rakuhoku Church in the A.M. and at the English service in the P.M. In addition, 21 young people of Rakuhoku came to our home for Bible study in the evening. I have moved my other Bible class to Thursday evening to meet the request of these Church young people.

Ayako-san has not been able to get her husband to attend church or Bible class although he has expressed a little interest in learning English. Her marriage was arranged by her parents and his but with their consent, the usual custom in Japan. Their parents told them they played together as children, but neither of them remembered so they came together practically as strangers who had to get used to one another.

Young people are independent in many ways now and I wonder why this custom is so hard to change. Maybe it has some merits we are not aware of. In a recent book, *Popcorn on the Ginza*, one girl is quoted as saying: "I could not trust myself to pick out as good and reliable a husband as my parents would choose for me."

We went to see the house in Nagano-cho yesterday and it will be O.K. with the new kitchen we will build with the owners' permission. Mr. Hayakawa can speak English but his wife cannot. Two maids welcomed us at the door and the wife finally appeared and seems friendly although a bit strained and stiff with us. She seems to be a strong-willed person and indicated she did not want to give up all her storage space she had been using in the apartment. We assured her we could probably make out all right with her keeping part of the storage space and this seemed to please her.

They have a boy about 14 and a girl about 12 and we want to have a good relationship with all of them. We know they are not Christians and seem to have little interest in religion beyond following traditional customs about festivals.

We had missed lunch so we appreciated the tea and candy she served us about one P.M. On our way back to Kyoto we managed to get a sandwich about four P.M. at the train's snack bar. We took a battery-operated taxi home which was so small we sat with legs doubled up under us. The battery has to be changed every two-and-a-half hours. Fortunately it had enough "juice" to get us home. This is one step up from the tourist rickshaw we saw in Kobe.

May 27, 1951

It is raining so hard we thought the rainy season (*nyubai*) had started but we were told it usually doesn't come until mid-June and is a light, steady rain that continues for about a month.

Friday we went to the Kabuki Theatre and saw four plays. The first lasted two hours, the second was very brief and the third and fourth were about an hour each. We entered at four thirty and got out at nine forty-five P.M. We took sandwiches for supper, although the Japanese usually buy box lunches sold at the theatre. The scenery and costumes were beautiful and the acting was very good in the first play which was a serious drama about life in the Tokugawa period. The comic play failed to overwhelm us with laughter. The ancient classical language is used throughout and even some Japanese people fail to understand it.

We understood very little of the language but could follow parts of the stories through the acting and by use of a written guidebook. The women's parts are all played by men and done quite well. Watching the audience we discovered that the usually reserved Japanese people seem to feel unrestrained to laugh or cry in a theatre. Perhaps that is one way they can find release from the impassive formality outside.

Yesterday the Ibuki family who are sponsoring the Thursday Bible Class took us to Nara for the day. They paid travel expenses and treated us to a tasty Japanese lunch of chicken and egg on rice (*Oyako domburi*).

Nara was the nation's capital before Kyoto and the temples are built of huge polished timbers with no paint and seem quite drab in contrast to some of the colorful temples and shrines in Kyoto. We saw the largest statue of Buddha in Japan—53½ feet high—in what we are told is the largest wooden building in the world, at least the largest of that style, having few pillars to support the large high roof. At one temple we got to ring a massive temple bell for the fee of ¥10 (3¢). You do this by swinging a log suspended on ropes until it hits the bell, ringing with a deep mellow tone.

We passed endless souvenir shops. Japan has learned how to make its tourist trade pay off. The most impressive sight to me was the herds of deer (*shika*) which are believed to be a messenger of Shinto deities and even though people were starving near the end of the war only one or two deer were ever poached for food. For 30¢ you can buy whole grain cookies to feed the deer. Sometimes tourists think the cookies are for people but they are always stopped from eating them by someone telling them, "no, no, no . . . Bambi."

Among the Japanese with us there Mrs. Ibuki is the only Christian—a wonderful and charming woman—who is praying her husband will be converted through the Bible class in their home. She was concerned to note Lillian's cold had passed on to seven-month old Edward who was wheezing. Medication from the doctor cleared his severe cold up in a few days, but Mrs. Ibuki went out of her way to tell us where we could buy long stockings to keep him warm. She has a ten-year-old son and a seven-year-old daughter and is very good with children.

June 3, 1951

Last Tuesday the furniture we wanted in Kyoto arrived

from the ship in Kobe. Although it was exam week at language school, we managed to unpack the most necessary things. I was so excited at getting my projector that I stayed up until after midnight looking at some of the slides I had accumulated of life in Japan.

Lillian learned from Mrs. Mori that you always serve tea and cookies to delivery-persons in a case like this. Her language study is a little more flexible than mine as she has a private tutor coming to the home. This allows her to care for baby Edward while continuing her studies. She likes her tutor, Takashima-sensei, who is a lovely person as well as a talented teacher. Lillian has been chosen to introduce her to a new student, Mrs. Wenger, which Japanese etiquette requires. It would be unthinkable for Takashima-sensei to go directly to the Wenger home without a formal introduction first.

Friday our language school group went to Otsu for a boat ride around beautiful Lake Biwa, one of Japan's largest lakes. The most enjoyable part of this picnic outing occurred for me when we stopped at a scenic island and climbed to the top of a high hill crowned by a historic Shinto shrine. Every time we got on the boat we had to take our shoes off and sit on the straw mats provided, but by now we are accustomed to removing our shoes in such cases. We got back to Otsu about 4 P.M. which got us home to Kyoto about five.

Yesterday I got Lillian's bicycle unpacked and reassembled and with Edward strapped into a baby seat on my Japanese bike we went for a ride along the Kamo River in Kyoto. It was a thrill to see the colorful strips of newly dyed cloth spread along the riverbank to dry.

June 9, 1951

We went downtown Tuesday to register at the army headquarters which is still necessary although the army influence is gradually giving way to Japanese control. Japanese law requires us to carry alien registration cards stating that our purpose in being here is quite different from that of the army.

Our new Lutheran friends, Gene and Dorothy Wenger,

had a bad week with their nine-month-old, Bonnie Gail, sick with dysentery and a fever of 104°. Our missionary doctor, Dr. Swearsenz, is in the hospital himself with a hernia so they had to call another doctor, but the baby has improved. Lillian visited them this afternoon.

When I come home tired from a day trying to communicate with Japanese people, Lillian says I carry over some Japanese language habits in my English such as saying "so desu" and "nee" which is the way many Japanese punctuate their remarks. Wayland Davis, an air force sergeant who is a cousin by marriage, has been visiting us for a few days and Lillian says I even said "so desu nee" to him. Maybe I am beginning to "internalize" some Japanese speaking habits.

I find that imitating others is one of the best forms of language study. After all, that is how we first learn to speak our own native tongue. In our language school we have students from Wales, Norway, Sweden, Finland, Australia and the U.S. representing six denominations and several mission boards. In my Bible class I have the honor of teaching two of Kyoto's most skilled technicians, an X-ray expert and a research chemist. The Japanese almost idolize a scientist, so we know the tremendous influence these two could have on others if they become Christians—which is our prayer. They already know more about the Bible than other members of the class.

June 24, 1951

Mr. Tominosuke Hayakawa, our landlord when we move to Nagano, has sent us an estimate of $300 to remodel the small Japanese style kitchen in our new apartment. It seems exorbitant to us but Mr. Hannaford approved the cost. The repairs include extending the kitchen roof and walls, putting in a sink and water pipes. Our new address from late July will be 565 Nagano-cho Minami Kawachi-gun, Osaka-fu, Japan.

The official rainy season began on the 17th, but it has not been too bad so far. In fact the misty rain and cloudy days bring a welcome relief from the heat that is becoming increasingly uncomfortable. However the high humidity makes the heat oppressive on sunny days, endless flooded rice fields and ponds provide moisture. There are several names for the rainy season, including *nyubai* and *tsuyu*.

July 8, 1951

Tonight was our last Bible class before moving to Nagano-cho and in spite of the rain, we had a good attendance. The members made it a sort of farewell party for us, but we still had to provide the refreshments as we meet in our home.

We have had to continue our inoculations for sleeping sickness and typhoid which are provided by the army hospital. However, being under Japanese law we ran into a little problem. It is illegal for us to own U.S. dollars or military script now, but we were supposed to pay one dollar for the shots. We solved the problem by having our bill sent to the interboard committee in Tokyo which handles any dollar expenses for us.

Edward took the first shot calmly but yelled a loud protest to the second one, as did a lot of other babies there, the worst being Dr. Swearsenz's little girl. She is old enough to remember what it was like from the last time.

July 18, 1951

Last Friday I began my climb of Mt. Fuji with school friends. Lillian went on to Zushi for a visit with Pearl and Dick Drummond.

Climbing Mt. Fuji was quite an adventure. Not only was it much more strenuous than we expected (my left knee will never be the same) we got caught in a violent rain and wind storm at the eighth station for two nights and one full day. We ran out of food but were able to buy rice and eggs from the caretakers of the hut there near the mountaintop.

The wind was so strong it would bowl us over if we went outside without holding on to the hut. One of the girls in our group got a bad case of "mountain sickness" when we got to an altitude of 10,000 feet. During the night Dr. Abe's daughter, quite an attractive girl, had to fight off the unwanted attentions of one of the caretakers of the hut who tried to force his way into her sleeping bag. She's a spunky young lady and handled this crisis without calling out for help.

Finally the weather cleared somewhat and we went on to the 12,388 foot summit. With fog and clouds blowing past us and nothing but multicolored volcanic rock around us we felt like we were treading the outskirts of hell. However, the view from the top was magnificent. Between drifting clouds we could see far off peaks and even occasional glimpses of blue ocean in the distance. Even the girl who got altitude sickness was glad she came. It required eight hours of climbing to reach the summit but only four hours to descend to the nearest bus stop.

Since I was a day late reaching the Drummonds' home where Lillian was waiting—with no way of letting them know we were trapped near the top—they were quite concerned. My glowing reports of the unusual scenery, a colorful Shinto shrine at the summit, snow banks still left at the higher elevations in July, helped them share in the adventure and forget the anxiety I had caused them. I did not arrive until near midnight and we stayed up until the wee hours talking.

For the Japanese, climbing Mt. Fuji is like visiting Mecca for the Muslims. I saw some of that in the thousands of worn-out straw sandals abandoned along the way (the sacred footgear) plus the well kept Shrine at the summit. But we did not meet many pilgrims along the way as they were smart enough to avoid the severe weather we endured. As one wise man said; "One who does not climb Mt. Fuji once is a fool. One who climbs it twice is a greater fool."

Although I was not a pilgrim in the Japanese Shinto sense, I did have my walking stick branded with the official symbol at each of the ten "stations" along the way which drew many admiring glances as I carried the stick on the train to Zushi.

While waiting for me at Zushi, a popular resort, Lillian and Edward enjoyed two swims in the ocean with the Drummonds. Lillian said nine-month-old Edward didn't like the cold water but relished digging in the black sand. He would walk slowly when going toward the water but ran when headed back to the sand.

Zushi is near the big Naval base of Yokosuka which has thousands of the world's sailors (mostly Americans) coming and going each day. The Drummonds report that sailors are served by 60,000 Japanese prostitutes which created many problems for their church. Local farmers send their daughters in to get money and don't seem to feel there is anything wrong about it. International marriages are also quite common in their church.

Lillian helped Dick in the wedding of a 17-year-old Japanese girl to a 23-year-old American sailor on Sunday, a few hours before I returned from Mt. Fuji. The couple had been living together for about a year and the girl claimed to have had no relationship with any other man. All went well with the ceremony except that the usher was too zealous and tried to usher the bride down the aisle even though her uncle was already doing the job, as the person who "gave her away."

July 21, 1951—Nagano-cho

We came to Nagano-cho today and found all is ready for us to move in except a bit more work which is needed to finish the kitchen—which we hope will be done by July 30th, the day we expect to arrive. We were given a royal welcome by a crowd of church children and leaders who met us at the train station. I stayed at the church for a night meeting and Lillian preceded me back to Kyoto. I will stay overnight and get as many of our things into the apartment tomorrow as time and space will allow.

July 27, 1951

Yesterday we packed all day in Kyoto and today we unpacked in Nagano-cho. Monday we move. I am staying overnight here again as I have to preach at a neighboring church tomorrow. Lillian didn't feel up to staying, with all the excitement of new people and places, but she does like the new apartment. She is also pleased to find she can get into the

big city of Osaka by a 50-minute ride on an electric train. The
large department store, Takashimaya, is located in the Namba
Station complex. With a 15-minute ride on the new subway,
she can shop at three more department stores: Daimura, Sogo
and Hankyu.

II

Early Problems and Promises

Aug. 5, 1951—Nagano-cho

Finally we are getting settled in our Japanese-style apartment at our appointed field of service to God and God's people in Nagano-cho. The 17,000 people living here, plus the tens of thousands in surrounding towns and villages, present quite a challenge to us.

Nagano-cho literally means "Long Field Town," and is named for a series of long fields stretching back from the banks of the Ishikawa River. A few homes grace the riverbank on the east side; however, they are limited to the few level spots found along the river and to the narrow valleys between the hills and mountains which rise abruptly from the river.

Mountains extend eastward as far as the eye can see. A scenic town park, displaying a profusion of cherry blossoms in spring, covers the flat top of the high hill which begins at the edge of our yard. Most of the homes, shops and factories are located on the west side of the river and are built on a gentle slope which rises gradually to an elevated plateau which has plenty of room for houses and farms. In land area, Nagano-cho is one of the largest towns in the Osaka Prefecture, but in population it is one of the smallest. The main function of the town is to serve the shopping, educational, social and political needs of the people living in the environs.

We have already told the story in the prologue of Monday our moving day when baby Edward fell out of an upstairs window in our new apartment. By God's grace we are recovering from that shock. We are also thankful that we now know more about our new friends at Nagano Church who were so helpful on that traumatic day.

One interesting fact about the members of Nagano Church is that two of the leading men were adopted into their families to carry on the family name where there was no male heir to do so. Mr. Konishi, who along with his wife and all three children are Christians, inherited from his adopted family a big home and much farm land where he grows grapes which he takes into Osaka and sells through the Takashimaya Department Store's supermarket. Those not good enough for sale as table grapes are made into wine which is used for communion services at the local churches. All churches in Japan use real wine, rather than grape juice, for their communion services.

Mr. Hosokawa, the other man adopted to carry on the family name, is the only Christian in his family. He works for a small factory here.

Noboru Nakayama, who founded Seikyo Gakuen Christian School in cooperation with Shinichi Ueda, has a sister who is adopted. She was an orphan, but Noboru's parents hesitated to adopt her because Noboru is their only son and there is a Japanese superstition that if a child is adopted into a family with only one son, he will die. It is a tribute to their Christian faith that they overcame this superstition and adopted this orphan girl.

Aug. 12, 1951

Yesterday and today we have been sharing in a study and fellowship retreat for the Nagano Church and the Tomioka Church which have their own small buildings plus two house church groups from Tondabayashi and Hatsushiba. Even though I understand only about half of what goes on I feel the warm fellowship of kindred Christian spirits which transcends language. We sing, pray and do Bible study together as well as discuss plans as to how to strengthen the groups in this area and reach out to neighbors with the good news of God's love for all people.

There is a spiritual hunger among many which has reached almost a crisis stage, for some Japanese believe that losing the war means that the old gods and religions of Japan have failed them. Although I cannot communicate well in their language they seem to appreciate the efforts I make and perhaps listen more carefully, and sympathetically, than if I were more skilled.

Lillian got lost coming out today by bicycle to the rural area where the retreat was being held, but she was proud to report that her language was good enough to ask directions and finally find her way. It is very hot and muggy here and Lillian says she almost gave up when she came upon the second big hill she had to climb. But the exertion she had to make to get there, and to speak the language, made her presence all the more appreciated by our new Christian friends and coworkers. Informally we used our limited Japanese in discussion groups, but for my formal presentation on Biblically based evangelism and for Lillian's on Christian education, Pastor Toru Hashimoto translated for us.

After getting used to 20-minute sermons in the U.S. it takes a bit of mental (and physical) adjustment to get accustomed to the hour-long sermons Japanese pastors usually preach. It is a lesson in patience as well as in Christian doctrine—to say nothing of the religious terms of this new language.

Aug. 26, 1951—Lake Nojiri in Nagano Prefecture

Our summer vacation at this lovely mountain lake is proving most relaxing and enjoyable. The lake is about one-and-a-half miles wide and three miles long, nestled in a valley surrounded by high mountains on three sides. The lower part of the mountains are heavily wooded but Mt. Myoko and Kurohime (black princess) are so high and cold at the summits that only scrub brush grows there. This is a summer resort started by missionaries a few years ago and now frequented by over 250 missionaries from all over the world, including many nations and denominations. Many Lutherans from the Scandinavian countries come here as it reminds them of mountains and lakes back home.

The fellowship, study and worship together is marvelous. The cabins are simple ones built for summer use only, very rustic with plain unpainted wood and snow pits for refrigerators. These are made by digging a deep hole into the side of the hill we live on. The pit is filled with snow in the winter and it never melts all summer. A crude door is fixed at the entrance and a rough wooden platform holds the food to be refrigerated just above the snow packed beneath it. Sometimes the snow is so heavy in the winter that it will break a roof in if it is not shoveled off. The Japanese caretakers who build the cabins and take care of them are all local people, very friendly and helpful. This summer vacation group provides extra income for them which they need and appreciate.

Since we are new and have no cabin yet (though we hope to buy one in a year or two) we stayed with Pearl and Dick Drummond upon arrival here late in the evening Monday. We had left Nagano before dawn by a car rented from our landlord's business company to catch an early morning train.

After spending three days with the Drummonds, Pearl was diagnosed by a missionary doctor as having a touch of T.B. so we moved in with the Howard Hannafords, whereupon hangs a tale.

The Hannafords borrowed a rowboat from the Thurbers to row us over to the small island in the lake for a picnic. It was a very windy day with high waves and the overloaded boat sank about 100 yards short of the island. Lillian and I are good swimmers and had our swim suits on so it was no big deal for us. However, the Hannafords were fully dressed and to her swimming credit, Mrs. Hannaford never lost the huge hat she had on, looking like a small snow-capped island in the water. The big shocker was to learn after he hit the water that Dr. Hannaford couldn't swim! Fortunately a friend was nearby with a boat and we had him hang on to our overturned boat until he could be rescued.

Lillian treaded water with our baby in her arms until he too was put in the rescue boat with the Hannafords, then we swam to shore pushing the up-side-down boat ahead of us. I felt terrible at having dunked the head of our mission but the only complaint he made was that his wallet and money got wet. We lost no time in buying him a new wallet the very next day.

For my birthday on Aug. 18th we had a more successful outing. The Davis family made secret plans for our Presbyterian "D" contingent (Daub, Davis, Driskill, Drummond) to go to the nearby Nojirko Hotel for a celebration dinner. What a wonderful time of sharing and fun it was. Of the Presbyterian "D's" only Dick Drummond was missing as he had to go to Tokyo to get some special medicine for Pearl. Late that night as we wended our way home, the moon made a path across the lake and I was thrilled at the beauty of God's creation, as well as the kindness of God's people who had entertained us. For several more days we enjoyed the fellowship and the swimming. Edward shows no fear of the water even though he got submerged when the boat sank.

Sept. 2, 1951—Nagano-cho
We are back home and the work is beginning to pile up. Even though we are supposed to spend half our time the first year here in language study, this is in danger of being crowded out. I am preaching and teaching regularly on Sundays as well as weekdays, and Lillian is beginning to use her Christian Education training. This afternoon for a couple hours a group of church school teachers were at our home and Lillian was the great teacher at whose feet they sat. They were most appreciative and asked that such a training session be planned at our home at least once a month.

Hungry for news from home, I sat up past midnight last night trying to get U.S. stations on my new shortwave radio and finally tuned in both Los Angeles and San Francisco.

Yesterday Lillian was washing her hair in the bathroom sink when a long, thin snake crawled up from the drain. As it "was not like any I had ever seen before as it had some queer headdress that made me think of a witch doctor!" Lillian reported later, she poured water down the drain which made it retreat temporarily. Lillian screamed when it came up again and our young girl helper, Shigeko Okuda, trembling all the time, rescued her by grabbing it with a wad of paper and throwing it out the window into the river. As usual in such a crisis I was not at home. Lillian's estimation of her heroine Shigeko-san climbed 100%. She is a jewel who takes good care of us even though she does tend to spoil Edward.

Being lenient with all children of preschool age seems to be a trait of the Japanese, but when they start to school discipline is imposed mercilessly. One would think that this sudden change from coddling to strict control would do psychological damage, but Japanese parents say, "a child needs freedom to grow without restraint in the first years but when school starts that is the time to replace self-interest with conformity to the larger welfare of the family and society."

Their philosophy is that from the first year, a school child must study diligently so as to be able to advance to the best high school, the best college and get a job with the best company. Sometimes competition to enter the best college is more than ten to one. Failing, even for entrance into a good high school, may provoke a suicide attempt. Before we condemn this pressure to excel, however, we must remember that Japan is a land with few natural resources which must live by its wits. As someone said, "Our only natural resource is people."

Sept. 16, 1951

Our new home is in a beautiful natural setting. The concrete basement wall of our apartment forms one bank of a sizable river and the other side of our house faces a small mountain that rises rapidly some thousand feet to a city park near the top. The main part of this small town of 17,000 is built on another hill across the river from us. The hill gradually climbs to a plateau which stretches for a mile or more beyond the center of the town to small farms of flooded rice fields which soon give way to more hills dotted with pictur-esque pine trees. A few Japanese-style inns and brothels line the riverbank to the east of us. A large Buddhist temple roof looms on the hill beyond the river. Cherry trees, dogwood and pines cover the mountainside leading to the city park.

Less than a block from our apartment is one of the endless wayside shrines to the Shinto god Inari who is supposed to insure good crops, family health and community protection. The fox is considered Inari's messenger and there are several ceramic fox figures on each side of the stone-carved image of the god. Daily elderly women come there to pray, bringing bowls of rice and cups of tea for the god, as well as flowers. Some worshippers, obviously under stress, pray fervently swaying back and forth in a sort of hypnotic trance. We watched from a discreet distance one tall, thin lady do this for some time and wondered what she was praying for.

Minor problems vex us almost daily. Edward has been waking each morning with tiny red spots on his skin. Shigeko-san says it is fleas from the landlady's dogs which apparently lodge in the straw *tatami* floor mats. Under her guidance we removed the finely woven straw matting which covers the heavier straw mat, then threw out the old newspapers from under them and took the heavy six by three foot mats outside to beat the dust out of them—creating quite a dust storm. Next we washed the floor, waited for it to dry, put down new pa-per and insecticide and replaced the mats and covering.

Just two rooms took three of us working all day from early morning till seven at night. No wonder they do it only once a year—or less if they get too busy—but it does seem to help.

We found old newspapers spread under the mats, includ-ing some old English editions published in Japan during the war. It is quite a shock to see headlines such as "AMERICAN ENEMY SMASHED AT PEARL HARBOR," "U.S.A. IS NO MATCH FOR THE INVINCIBLE FORCES OF JAPAN," "SOLDIERS GLADLY GIVE THEIR LIVES FOR THE EMPEROR," "VICTORY IS ASSURED."

Another vexation are big river rats which eat our potatoes

and gnaw through our food storage boxes. We set traps and two nights ago caught a huge rat, about ten inches long. Last night Lillian wakened me saying, "I can hear a rat gnawing right beside our bed." I put on the light but couldn't find anything. I agreed to set another trap under our bed.

Mosquitoes breed in swarms in the flooded rice fields and along the river. They make our nights miserable even though we shut all the doors and windows despite the heat. After being driven wild several nights we finally bought nets to sleep under and can sleep again.

The city water system is being repaired and should be O.K. by October but in the meantime our water supply is a sometime thing. Electricity rationing is even worse. It is turned off three days a week now—Monday, Wednesday and Friday. Almost every night it is off for 20 minutes out of every hour after dark. We are learning to live with candlelight, just like our pioneer ancestors did. With refrigeration limited, we have to do food shopping almost daily, as the Japanese have always done. Housewives seem to like daily shopping as it is an opportunity to get out of the house and chat with friends at the market.

To get hot water we are fixing up a Japanese style heater—a tank in the ground with a firebox attached which you draw up and build a fire in and then let down again. The main problem is having enough wood. We still have to heat water for most purposes on the kerosene stove. Kerosene is stored in a large barrel outside our front door with a faucet on it.

We discovered the only way to flush our toilet is to pour water down it. It is simply a holding tank with an overflow exit which I am beginning to suspect eventually seeps into the river. This could be a serious health hazard, although our landlord assures us it is not! At least it is less smelly than the usual Japanese small tank toilets which need to be emptied every few days and carted to the fields as fertilizer.

The buckets used to haul it are euphemistically called "honey buckets." At the field the human waste is stored in large open holes in the ground. One of our missionary kids fell into one of them and survived only because a passing Japanese lady saw him fall and rescued him in time. No feared disease followed, though it was quite a job to get the mess out of his ears, nose, mouth and hair.

We are grateful that God has enabled us to adjust to this new life in Japan as some missionaries we know were not able to do so and had to return home. One young missionary, Bert Houseman, insisted on living as the Japanese do and has damaged his eyes seriously with trachoma which he probably caught by taking his daily baths at the local public bath where the dark, damp conditions encourage the growth of bacteria and germs. It is not unusual to see a child with a bandage over one eye. Fortunately, his three-year contract as a teacher in Seikyo Gakuen is now ending and he can return to the U.S. for the best treatment available. Lillian and I will take over several of his English conversation classes.

Sept. 23, 1951

Cleaning the straw *tatami* mats following the Japanese method has paid off. Edward's flea bites seem to have disappeared and maybe he won't get any more now. We also discovered a couple of broken porch railings which must be replaced before Edward takes a 15-foot tumble into the river flowing by our house. He is now learning to climb the steep stairs to the second floor and we plan to put up a protective railing and a gate at the top. To save space, Japanese stairs are much steeper than those in America and precautions are needed. Falls on these stairs by young and old are not uncommon.

Electricity is in short supply here. We have such frequent stoppages that we never sit down at night without a candle and matches nearby. Recently the lights have been going out on the hour so we have some idea of when to be ready for it. The newspapers now speak of the possibility of a strike in the coal mines so this may mean many extra hours without electricity.

Sept. 30, 1951

Our rat problem continues. The other night one ate the binding off our Sears catalogue stored in a closet. Right after that we were awakened by what sounded like a horse in the kitchen. We haven't much hope of getting rid of them completely since about half our closet space is used by the Hayakawas and we can't clean it out. Also since this house adjoins the Hayakawa home, rats can move easily from one to another. We have finally gotten a three-month-old kitten to try to scare the rats off. Unfortunately the cat also scares our landlady. I found that she was born in the "year of the rat" and is therefore superstitiously terrified by cats. However, not much else scares or intimidates her, including her husband.

She runs the home with an iron hand, including complete control of the finances, daily affairs of the household and children. She gives her husband an allowance for train fare and incidentals and always pays the bills when they eat out at a restaurant. Although Japan is supposed to be a "man's country" this is not true in the home. He still has control of "major decisions" but most wives like Mrs. Hayakawa see to it that a "major decision" almost never occurs.

This small "iron lady" even tries to control us by often opening our adjoining door (locked on her side) without warning to check up on how the foreign renters are doing. We confess to an unholy joy when one day she suddenly opened the door on us and our cat dashed through making her shudder with fright. Otherwise she is quite likeable so we quietly endure the intrusions.

Incidentally, most husbands tell me they like their wives to control the finances and the home because this relieves them of the responsibility. Also handling money is considered by many men as beneath their dignity—a dirty business best left to the "weaker" sex.

Lillian is rejoicing that she found her favorite disinfectant, Lysol, available here. She went to a beauty parlor in the Takashimaya department store in Osaka and saw them putting utensils in a solution to sterilize them. When she asked what it was they said "rysol" (Japanese often confuse L and R). She happily bought some at the same department store drug counter.

Buying chicken was an adventure. At this same store Lillian had a difficult time convincing the clerk that she wanted them to clean out the insides (intestines and internal organs) rather than do it herself at home, as apparently many Japanese women do. But she finally got her point across with broken Japanese and sign language and they did a good job of cleaning it.

A week earlier she asked Shigeko-san to buy a chicken and the opposite happened—she came home with it all cut up in half-inch pieces, which is the way the Japanese use it in rice dishes such as *oyako domburi*. Each Saturday Shigeko-san prepares a full Japanese style dinner for us and we are finding them delicious.

Our Sunday service on September 30th fell into the usual pattern: Sunday school and worship service in the morning, Bible class for me in the afternoon and a special meeting at night for the youth where I showed the slides of church work in the U.S. and explained how some of our youth groups operate there. We have to meet with some school or church group almost every day but are trying to save Monday as our day off—even though this is not working too well.

Oct. 8, 1951

Doing without electricity much of the time is quite irritating. I got one side of my face shaved with my electric shaver the other morning and the electricity went off. I had to wait all day to finish shaving. Mrs. Hayakawa got part way through a permanent wave treatment at the beauty shop and had to come home only half done. A local butcher was working on his meat cutting machine when the electricity came back on suddenly and it cut off his hand. Last night it went off every 15 minutes which kept us busy lighting candles and blowing them out again. We will buy an oil lamp soon.

We are gradually becoming acquainted with the Japanese

religious customs here. Yesterday morning at eight Lillian and I were on our way to Sunday school when we saw holy men in black robes with a basket-like cover over their heads going from house to house playing a flute to chase away evil spirits. In gratitude the housewife is supposed to come out and make a monetary gift for their services, which they usually do. Older women chanting their prayers at wayside Shinto shrines and at Buddhist temples are becoming a familiar sight to us. Some sway back and forth in an ecstasy or frenzy of prayer, oblivious of all that goes on around them. My friends tell me that they are usually praying about some personal or family problem such as illness, family strife or economic need.

In addition to my work with the Seikyo Gakuen school, Lillian is now teaching three classes a week there. These junior high students are a lively lot, some genuinely interested in learning English with others interested only in goofing off, much like junior high students everywhere. It is satisfying to see them in good spirits with hope for the future after the humiliating defeat and near-starvation conditions during the last days of the war. Their bright spirits will help keep us young.

Oct. 14, 1951

The *Aki Matsuri* (Fall Festival) drums have been beating off and on since last Wednesday—almost four days of celebration for a good harvest and prayers for future blessings. Four large cart-like vehicles are pulled along the street with a man inside beating the drum. The children love it, as do many adults. At night huge decorative lanterns adorn the cart on all sides and it is a beautiful sight to see. In addition to this colorful moving attraction, booths selling candy, good luck charms, clothing, food and drink of all kinds line the streets.

It is quite a spectacle. A magician awed people with his tricks and we bought a little man made of straw from him. There is a point on the end of one foot and if you stick the point into the crease of the palm of your hand you can make the man stand up or lie down without apparently moving him. Unfortunately the point hit Edward's balloon and burst it at which he complained loudly. The candy we bought didn't seem sweet at all, it was more like peanuts than candy. The constant beating of the drums can get on one's nerves until you get used to it.

Now in addition to the days when we have no electricity, it goes off for two hours out of every four on other days. Sometimes it seems it might be better not to have it at all, but when it goes on again we are always happy to have it. Our wood-burning hot water heater seems to work better now that we know how to operate it more effectively so there is plenty of hot water for baths, washing our hair and washing dishes.

Oct. 21, 1951

Two tiny girl babies were born to our Japanese friends this past week. Mrs. Hayakawa had a doctor in attendance but Pastor Hashimoto's wife chose a midwife, a member of our church here. When we went to see them, each mother was on a *futon* (cotton-padded quilts) on the floor with the baby on a small *futon* beside the mother, all bundled up so she couldn't move. It is interesting that although one mother is rich and has helpers and the other is poor, they still seemed to live in similar style, sleeping on the floor.

The *futon* is the Japanese bed and is simply huge padded quilts brought out of the closet each night and put on the straw mat floor then folded up each morning and put away. Their pillows are made of a hard cloth bag filled with chaff and being hard and small we find it difficult to get used to. When we are at church conferences or at Japanese inns, we sleep on *futons*, but I usually substitute two small cushions for the hard pillow.

Edward's first birthday on Oct. 18th was quite an occasion, although we tried to keep it simple. After breakfast he looked at his gifts and I took some pictures of him playing with toys. He was so exhausted by all the excitement he slept soundly for his morning nap and then again in the afternoon.

Lillian had baked a cake and made ice cream in the morning to prepare for the expected guests. Tsujino-sensei (a Seikyo

Gakuen teacher) and his small daughter were the first guests to arrive that afternoon. Soon after this, Pastor Hashimoto showed up with his small son, Mitsuru-chan. His wife and her sister came a little later bringing a large rubber fawn, Bambi, for Edward. The Tsujino girl, Sayuri-chan, brought a large traditional Japanese doll carrying rice. These historical dolls are quite famous in Japan but are encased in glass and are only to look at. I recorded the event in slides.

Our Sunday supper was a box lunch given to me by one of the ladies at the church where I preached. It is a colorful combination of *sushi* which is made up of rice balls topped with fish, both cooked and raw types. I eat the raw, but Lillian eats only the cooked. It is really quite tasty when done properly using the spicy sauce provided for it.

Oct. 28, 1951

We have helped with five church meetings today; Sunday school this morning, church at ten, my Bible class in the afternoon plus a teacher's meeting in our home. Then I preached at an evening meeting in a nearby town. I am over my cold, but Lillian has a stomach upset which I think is due to all the excitement, but she thinks it is from eating bad food in a recent visit to Osaka.

We buy ice cream mix and make it in our refrigerator so the treat today is peppermint ice cream, Lillian's favorite which tastes good even with the upset. Japanese people are not used to heated houses and dress too warmly to be comfortable where there is much heat. Therefore we keep the heat down when we have guests and this is hard on our colds. Because of the high humidity in Japan the winter cold is a damp, clammy type that penetrates to the bone no matter how many layers of clothing we put on. The Japanese think we are crazy to complain of the cold and still eat ice cream in winter.

The Japanese theory is that if your hands are warm your whole body will be warm. Therefore, all you need to keep warm is a *hibachi*, a small ceramic pot with glowing charcoal over which the hands are warmed. I can testify the theory doesn't work, especially when you must use your hands away from the charcoal for typing, cleaning or almost any work. Yet this is the only type of heat most Japanese homes have. However, at night most homes light up the *kotatsu* which helps the school kids to keep their feet warm while studying. This is a pit in the floor covered over with a low table with a quilt arranged over it to keep in the charcoal heat. By sitting on the edge of the pit with the feet dangling over the charcoal and the quilt tightly tucked around the waist four people can use the table for study or work and at least keep their feet warm.

This is a step up from the *hibachi* warming the hands but is still a far cry from a heated room, which is found only in a few public buildings such as the big department stores. Small shops usually have only a *hibachi* and vegetable and fruit stalls are usually in the open air even when it is snowing. These have no front walls, only three walls and a roof with the front open. It makes a convenient, colorful display case but provides little comfort for the customer (or the storekeeper).

In the markets we can buy mandarin oranges, apples, spinach, green beans, potatoes, melons, bananas, eggs, meats of all kinds, bread, canned pineapples, canned salmon, fresh fish of all kinds, eggplants, cabbage and tomatoes. The foods we miss are celery, lettuce and lemons, but we can buy even those in Osaka.

Nov. 11, 1951

Young people often ask to visit our home to learn English or inquire about America or Christianity so we have started a weekly open house on Tuesday nights which we hope to keep up indefinitely, for we feel this is an important aspect of our work. We are busy with language study (four days a week for me and three for Lillian) plus our church responsibilities, but these informal contacts will reach people who would not ordinarily come to a church meeting—and we are making many new friends this way.

One of our first visitors was a young man who is gradually going blind. In my poor Japanese I tried to comfort and help him as best I could, but I felt I was too unskilled in Japanese to console him on a spiritual level. Daily we see why it is so important to perfect our language skills. These are matters of life and death, hope or despair and we must be better prepared both spiritually and linguistically.

Having one-year-old Edward with us opens many doors into the lives and hearts of Japanese people. His blond hair intrigues the black-haired Japanese—children and adults alike. They love to feel his hair and touch his pink skin. Fortunately he doesn't seem to mind since he came to Japan at the age of four months and knows this culture better than the one he was born into. He loves to sing at church but always begins with the organ not waiting for the congregation, which wins tolerant smiles from others. With no heat in most places we take Edward, our chief concern is putting enough clothes on him to keep him warm. Fortunately he is very active and generates a lot of his own heat.

Our preaching station at Tondabayashi had a setback with the landlord refusing to continue to rent our meeting place to us. He says the reason is the noise the Sunday school children make, but I suspect he is also under pressure from neighbors of this strongly Buddhist town objecting to his renting property to Christians.

The prejudice is subtle but manifest. Often our signs and handbills advertising special meetings are taken down and disappear suddenly. I get irritated and discouraged. Lillian says I need more B vitamins to stabilize my nerves and make me easier to live with. I hope the vitamins plus God's grace will help brighten things up.

They say the first year on the mission field is the hardest and I can believe it. The strain of learning a new language and culture plus endless demands upon the "expert from overseas" takes its toll. Fortunately, Lillian and I both find that prayer, plus good nutrition, exercise and rest do help. At first I felt guilty even taking time for my private devotions when I should be out "helping people." However, I have finally realized that it is no use to "go out" if I have nothing spiritually helpful to give to others, or if I am not skilled enough in the language to communicate the insights God gives me to share with others.

I have decided that even language study and private devotions are "mission work" because they are essential in witnessing effectively to God's love in Christ Jesus. Therefore, I no longer feel guilty at taking time for my own private devotions. Fortunately all the walking I have to do helps with the exercise problem and we are working on the nutrition angle as well. Finding adequate time for rest with so many legitimate demands upon one's schedule is the biggest problem, but not insurmountable as we learn to put our priorities in proper order.

Lillian tends to have to cope with quite a few unexpected guests in the home. We had a famous 77-year-old evangelist, Dr. Logan, speak at our school and thought only one or two Japanese guests would show up to eat with him at our home. However, several unanticipated guests showed up, so Lillian had to hustle to feed them all.

This is not uncommon. Apparently people here love to eat in a foreigner's home and we are glad they feel welcome to do so, in spite of the strain it puts on our hospitality. It is helpful to discuss this with the other missionaries in the area when we get together in Osaka or Kobe for worship and fellowship about once a month. It is wonderful the way we all support each other with prayers, encouragement and help of endless kinds—no matter what the denominational difference.

Nov. 26, 1951

Shigeko-san just celebrated her 22nd birthday so we gave her a small birthday party last Saturday. Lillian had bought her a pink slip at the export bazaar. Shigeko-san put the gift beside her on an empty chair and pretended it wasn't there. After the meal we suggested she open it but she said in Japan the custom is not to open gifts until you get home. We said if she wanted, she could open it right then, American style, so she did. Lillian had learned from Ayako-san in Kyoto that girls here especially like pretty lingerie. Shigeko-san certainly seemed delighted with her gift.

It is getting quite chilly here now and we are amazed at how many Japanese children run around the cold wooden floors in church with nothing on their feet except thin socks, some even in bare feet. Apparently having bare feet seems to bother them little more than having bare hands.

Tadayoshi, our landlord's son, told me he is trying to make it into December with no socks on at all, to "toughen up his feet." As an active boy just entering his teens he must be better insulated than most adults for I notice that they wear fairly heavy socks in winter.

Our bedroom has no heat at all but we do put on heavy sheets and quilts and try to keep some heat in our living room and Edward's room, turning off the kerosene stoves in mid-day when it warms up enough to endure the cold. Our November afternoons warm up to about 50°, sometimes a little higher. It usually snows several times in the winter, I hear, but still it is not cold enough for anyone to freeze; therefore they build quite open houses with poorly fitting sliding doors. The resulting fresh breezes which blow through probably keep everyone from dying of monoxide poisoning from the small charcoal *hibachi* fires burning in each room.

In Hokkaido where it often gets below zero they apparently do have heated houses. In fact one visitor from Hokkaido told us he felt colder in Osaka with the open houses than in sub-zero Hokkaido's heated homes. I guess it is some comfort to know that in Osaka you don't freeze, you just feel miserable all winter long.

The Thurbers, our friends in Kyoto, are buying an electric blanket but Lillian doesn't like the idea so I guess we won't follow suit. I think she is afraid we might get electrocuted. But we are buying some warm, Japanese *futons* since we can use them for our guests, Jane and Roger Simpson, who plan to visit us the day after Christmas.

Edward likes our kerosene stoves so much he managed to push on the tank and get enough to smear on his face, which he did when my back was turned. I had to wash out his eyes with a boric acid solution. Fortunately there seemed to be no permanent damage. Because of our uncertain water supply we have to keep pails of water in the kitchen and it is taking quite a bit of patience to teach Edward he is not to play in the water. At one month past his first birthday he has finally learned to say "daddy" and a few other words.

Dec. 10, 1951

On December 2 we had Captain Mitsuo Fuchida, the converted leader of the Japanese Air Force group that attacked Pearl Harbor, here for a special evangelistic meeting. Many new people responded to our extensive publicity and came, including part of our landlady's family.

We are getting quite fond of this family of five and they seem to be responding well to us. How wonderful it would be if they would accept Christ as their Lord and Savior! While from a Buddhist background they seem to have little or no meaningful faith to help them in facing life's problems, including illness. In fact young Tadayoshi has had a very bad cold which kept him out of school for a week. Apparently by going without socks to "toughen up" his feet he overdid it and left his body open to a vicious cold bug that he ignored until he was forced to stay home.

Like many Japanese, the Hayakawa family feel that the old religions of Japan failed them when they got defeated in the war and they are reluctant to believe anything until they can be sure it is good for them and for Japan. In spite of the skepticism, however, I am finding that I have more opportunities to speak about God's love in Christ than I can adequately take care of.

Trying to take advantage of every opportunity I seem to be in danger of ruining my own health. Lillian is good at noticing the signs of stress and in reminding me that there are limitations to what one person can do. Maybe I need to reflect on what Peter Marshall said when asked what he learned when immobilized for three months by a heart attack: "I learned the Lord could get along without Peter Marshall."

Since Christmas is a busy time for the missionary community, we had a special fellowship and early Christmas celebration party last Saturday in Osaka with 150 missionaries of all denominations in attendance—including many children. Edward loved playing with other toddlers and kept us busy running after him. Lillian had a stomach upset but ate the delicious dinner anyway, resulting in her not being able to go to church yesterday.

My regular Bible class was recessed because of the school exams which are going on so I had time to help care for Edward part of the day. Our blatant commercialization of Christmas is done one better by the Japanese who see this as an economic bonanza. Christmas decorations and songs everywhere all center on "Santa Claus." It is discouraging to hear the true meaning of Christmas only in churches. However, I am optimistic that one day the Japanese will go beyond the hoopla and economics to investigate the true meaning of the coming of God's Son at Christmas.

We almost ran out of kerosene last night and are now waiting for the oil man to bring a new drum full. Fortunately we have enough left to keep the heater going until about noon tomorrow for in this kind of weather, with Lillian not feeling well, it would be unfortunate to run out completely.

Dec. 16, 1951

Today was hectic. I had to preach in the morning at the Tomioka church where I nearly froze because there was no heat in the church and it is considered impolite to preach with a top coat on. A sweater under my suit coat and two pairs of socks was just not enough to do the job. We hurried home for lunch and then took a 1:30 train to Osaka where I had to preach and conduct a communion service for the English-speaking congregation—mostly American missionaries and business people, plus some military families. The service was held in the army's Protestant chapel.

One of the women brought the communion set and we

brought the bread and grape juice. It was a rush to get it ready in time and then we learned we were expected to supply the organist as well. For awhile it looked like Lillian would have to take over but she was relieved when a capable substitute volunteered.

By next Sunday we all plan to put on our heaviest winter underwear, "long johns." That should help a little. We arrived this evening after six and found it was 40° inside. With the heater going full blast it made it up to 60° by bedtime.

Trains and stores are now mobbed with the holiday rush of Christmas and New Year's celebrations, with the latter being more important to the secular Japanese than is Christmas. Stores are busiest on Sundays and most are closed Mondays. We arrived home tired tonight but we still had all the dishes since breakfast to do plus boil water, as the tap water which only runs occasionally is still not considered safe to drink.

Shigeko-san has made her decision to be baptized at Christmas. She was examined and approved for baptism by the Japanese pastor—which is the rule for baptisms here. We are pleased and happy, especially since it is a difficult decision for her because her adoptive parents don't approve. Fortunately she is old enough to make her own decision so they can't prevent it. We hope they will soon change their minds as they see her happy in her new faith. I question her decision to keep it from them until later but I suppose she knows what is best in her particular situation.

Dec. 23, 1951

Today I spoke at three special Christmas programs. I have been preaching at least once a day since last Friday and the Christmas meetings will continue at least until the day after Christmas for a total of about a dozen meetings. Christmas is a golden opportunity to tell people about God's love in sending Jesus as our Savior and we try to make the most of every opportunity. Our morning worship and Christmas celebration at church went on for three hours and no one complained, in fact they seemed to enjoy the special atmosphere of witness, song and rejoicing. Maybe we American Christians need to do more celebrating.

The Hayakawas gave us a live turkey for Christmas. It is considered polite to do this as you will then know for sure it is fresh. I was away at meetings when it was delivered and Lillian and Shigeko-san wouldn't touch it. They left it in its box in our *genkan* (entrance) and I had to take it to the butcher for processing after I got home. Between the barking dogs outside, the yowling cats inside and the gobbling turkey in the genkan Edward had quite an exciting afternoon. Now the turkey is in our refrigerator waiting to be roasted Tuesday morning. We will have to start it very early as it is quite big.

The Hashimotos are coming to have dinner with us at 11:30 a.m. We have to eat early as Pastor Hashimoto and I both have an early afternoon meeting and Lillian will play another piano solo for the Christmas program at the school. I was also scheduled to speak Christmas night but Lillian asked that I beg off so we would have at least a little time together as a family on Christmas Day. I have a meeting Christmas Eve but will be home in time to trim the tree.

Shigeko-san was baptized today, along with ten other people—including six from Tondabayashi where I preach once a month. Since they have no fully organized church or church building they come under the jurisdiction of the church here in Nagano-cho. Mrs. Hashimoto's little girl was baptized and her mother wore a kimono while all the elders and the pastor wore tuxedo and tails. No matter how poor, every Japanese person must have one good kimono or tuxedo for such special occasions and they often sacrifice much to do so.

March 9, 1952

Today was Lillian's 40th birthday. I was up at six to prepare a special breakfast for her so when she came down the table was set with birthday napkins, a fruit bowl (with real oranges, huge apples and bananas) and candles. On Lillian's plate was a waffle lit with one pink birthday candle and her birthday gift in front of it. She reacted as if the waffle was a real birthday cake.

Edward has had chicken pox since Wednesday and the Thurbers had to cancel their planned visit with us because their son, David, is ill with what they think is "infectious mononucleosis." At one point his temperature reached 105.3°. Edward's fever is also high but lower than David's.

Our doctor, Dr. Sawada, diagnosed it as a cold at first but when he sent his sister, also a doctor, on our second call she diagnosed it as chicken pox, with spots all over Edward's body as proof. Friday night he slept fine until midnight and after that we had to take turns sitting up with him the rest of the night. By then the spots were even in his eyes and ears. He was a mess! And so miserable.

We tried a soda bath as suggested by Dr. Spock in his baby book. When we ran out of soda we tried starch and even boric acid powder. Saturday morning the doctor came again, gave him a second injection and left some medicine to apply once a day to his sores. His fever reached 104.5° yesterday and we gave him some aspirin finally to help him (and us) sleep that night. This morning, Sunday, he felt much better and I was able to give some attention to Lillian on her birthday.

After preaching at church I had Lillian stay in the living room while I prepared her birthday dinner. I had arranged for the Hashimotos to take the place of the Thurbers as her birthday guests and they arrived about one. I cooked sukiyaki right on the table (it is usually the man's job in Japan to cook sukiyaki—nothing else). In addition we had tai fish, the celebration fish which Japanese say is so good "it is even delicious when rotten."

Our language teacher, Tamura-sensei, a lovely single lady, had brought a big bowl of birthday rice (dyed red with food coloring) and Shigeko-san had also made some before leaving on Saturday. We will be eating rice for several days. Although it was her day off, Shigeko-san returned for the dinner. Lillian's gifts included a necklace and earrings, slippers, a *soroban* (abacus) and a Japanese game called *go*.

As a joke I brought out the waffle with one candle on it

for Lillian to blow out while Shigeko-san prepared the real birthday cake in the kitchen. It was two-layered covered with white icing with roses piled in the middle and twelve pink candles around it. It was a beauty, Shigeko-san's gift to Lillian. Her card was written in English, which was a real effort for her, and said: "I bless your birthday with all my heart. Thanks for your kind leading every day, and wish you many happy returns of the day. Love, Shigeko."

Lillian was deeply impressed. With the cake we had ice cream and black tea (we had green tea with the sukiyaki), followed by peanuts and candy. In spite of being exhausted from taking care of Edward, Lillian really enjoyed her birthday.

After hearing my morning sermon at church she said "It was your best sermon ever. With the English copy in my hand I could follow your Japanese quite well. I could tell you had the congregation right with you." That was a nice compliment to end a festive birthday celebration.

March 17, 1952

Taking part in the first graduation ceremony for the new school, Seikyo Gakuen, was quite an experience. It went on for five hours, including speeches, songs, a dinner together as well as the usual handing out of diplomas. As the related missionary, I had to give my speech, entertain with a song and share in all the festivities. Lillian had to dash home to prepare lunch for six people, three of whom had to leave on a 12:30 p.m. train.

Last night we folded, inserted and stamped 159 Christmas letters—but that is only about half. The rest need personal notes so we will be very busy with that the rest of the week.

Lillian is pregnant with our second child, which is due sometime in September. Since she lost so much blood when Edward was born we know we have to be near a hospital when the time comes and are considering going to the Seventh Day Adventist Hospital in Tokyo. We could rent housing from missionary friends who plan to be away then.

March 29, 1952

Lillian says one of the hardest things of being a missionary in Japan is not having other women to talk to in English so she really appreciated the recent visits of Dorothy Taylor and Dorothy Schmidt. She also plans to spend several days with Jane Simpson in Kobe while Roger and I attend the Interboard Conference in Tokyo the first of April. Jane says she is "going to talk Lillian to death" when she visits.

We have accepted the Drummonds' offer to sell us their old 1943 American Motors "Americar" for $400. I plan to bring it back from the Tokyo area after the April conference, picking it up in Kamakura on the way home from the conference. Getting a Japanese driving license wasn't easy. There is no English translation of the lengthy written exam so they read them to me and I answered them orally. I missed a few of the 20 questions but they were not critical ones so I got my license. Of course my U.S.A. license is still valid so that helped. They didn't require a driving test and I joked that they were afraid to trust me with one of their Japanese cars since I missed five of the questions. We had a problem finding a place to keep the car as the bridge across the river, and the road to our house, is too narrow to get a car through.

April 8, 1952

Lillian bought Edward a pair of overalls only to discover that the straps are too short while the trouser legs are plenty long. Maybe Japanese babies have shorter bodies than Caucasians. Anyway, Lillian will figure out some solution.

Driving the car from Tokyo was an adventure. Most of the trip was on dirt roads which are full of pot holes. Few Japanese own cars so they don't complain—only the truckers complain. We had to stop at three garages for repairs: the muffler fell off first, then the gears got stuck in high. No wonder Dick wanted only $400 for this car.

While waiting for repairs in one town Roger and I went to a local restaurant that was reputed to have Western food. We discovered it was more a brothel than a restaurant. After we had eaten a not-too-delicious meal the manager came up and discreetly asked if we were ready for the girls yet. We said "no," hid our shock and quietly slipped out soon afterward.

I felt really sorry for one young girl who waited on our table. Her genuine beauty was spoiled by the fact that she was almost too drunk to handle the dishes. It was my first good view of what a place like that could do to a young girl.

Being delayed by repairs, Roger took the train from Nagoya and I drove straight through to Nagano-cho without any more trouble.

April 20, 1952

We are finding that the car is a limited blessing here, not only because of the many repairs needed but also because of the bad roads which are mainly unpaved, narrow and filled with a mixed clientele of three-wheeled trucks, ox carts, bicycles and pedestrians all risking their lives as they vie for position. Since many children use the road for a playground this also is a peril. Yet the car is an advantage in getting to home church meetings in the surrounding towns and villages, as well as for an occasional shopping excursion to Osaka without having to carry Edward in our arms.

Japanese people are amazed to see a car like ours which has the gearshift on the steering wheel, as no Japanese cars have such. With no road to our house big enough for a car and no garage available, we have to park the car in front of the local train station. So far it has been safe.

Our choice of a lot to build a missionary house here has been approved by Dr. John Coventry Smith and the committee (Newton Thurber, Alice Grube, Ernest Chapman). Dr. Smith stayed overnight with us Saturday night and since I had to preach Sunday morning, Noboru Nakayama took him on the train to Osaka. The lot overlooks a green valley through which the main road and two commuter train lines run. There are wooded hills on the other side of the narrow valley and we have a great view of the city park and these rolling hills fading into the distance. While the valley is filled with homes and shops, the hills have few houses and many trees—pine and cherry plus bamboo. The cherry trees have been a profusion of blooms for several weeks, just ending now. The road beside the lot leads to a Buddhist temple, Gokurakuji, some two blocks away. Pastor Hashimoto tells us this land is so cheap and sparsely habited since Japanese avoid it because of their superstitions about the funeral processions that pass along it to the temple—so their fear of funerals has preserved this wonderful view lot for us to enjoy. How nice!

I have begun weekly meetings in Kaizuka, a textile city an hour's drive away by car. We meet every Wednesday in a small rented hall near the train station, which I have been paying for out of my work funds. Kaizuka is a city of 50,000 and most people work in the textile mills, other small factories or on the surrounding farms. There are about 30 Buddhist temples there with a small Shinto shrine visible at most road intersections but not a single Christian church.

It is reputed to be a famous red-light district for philandering men who come by train from Osaka to this seaside city. The name "Kaizuka" means "Shell Mound," and the sea shells abound on its white beaches. I was fascinated to watch a group of fishers pulling a heavy net containing many small fish. One elderly man with most of his teeth missing still managed to take one of the wriggling fish, bite off its head and chew it right on the spot.

I am learning to eat specially prepared raw fish (sashimi) but that seems a little too raw to appeal to me. I noticed not many others joined in eating the live fish. There is a teacher at the high school who is a Christian and is trying to interest students and others to attend our Wednesday night meeting.

One faithful Christian who has started coming regularly is Nabata-san, the owner and operator of a small box factory who works out of his home where he makes boxes for cakes, candy and other goods sold in local stores. Nabata-san is a thin, quiet man who became a Christian when witnessed to by visiting Christians in a tuberculosis hospital. He lost his wife many years ago and runs the shop himself with occasional hired help when big orders come in. He comes, listens, makes his offering and leaves with a contented look on his face, rarely saying more than hello and goodbye. There is something very appealing about him.

In addition to the colds that plague us in this damp climate, we have gotten intestinal parasites (worms) from eating Japanese food. Lillian is now taking medicine to eliminate them which should result in giving her more energy and less anemia which has shown up on recent tests.

May 12, 1952

Shigeko-san has had to leave us to rest for a couple of months for she has peritonitis. We learned that she was briefly married to a man chosen for her but this was annulled after a few days because her adoptive mother and her new husband couldn't get along together in the same house. Usually the bride goes to live with the groom's folks but since Shigeko-san is adopted the parents wanted also to adopt her new husband and make him their legal heir because they have no children of their own and need someone to carry on the family name (on the male side).

Shigeko-san's mother is an intelligent woman but she is very aggressive, critical and nervous—which may have added to the problem. Her father is just the reverse—one of the most calm, kindly and tranquil men we have ever met. We never met the rejected husband as this all occurred just before Shigeko-san came to work for us.

Yesterday we had the enjoyable experience of attending the wedding of my language teacher. The bride and groom wore Western dress but the maid of honor was in a kimono and *geta* (pretty wooden sandals). It is interesting how the Japanese are combining Western and Eastern customs. My teacher's home has both. He studies with a Western desk and chair, eats at a Western-style table but sleeps on a straw-mat floor. When I asked him which style he liked best, he answered, "I like what is convenient."

Most men wear Western suits during the day but upon

arriving home at night immediately change into a *yukata* (a kind of lounging robe). Western flush toilets are longed for, but I believe the Japanese hot tub bath will go on forever. It is much more relaxing than the Western shower or bath and, in winter, a good way to get warmed up before going to bed in an unheated room.

We were the only Westerners of some hundred guests at Yagi-sensei's wedding and I had the honor of giving the benediction. After the Christian service, the church was transformed into a reception room by curtaining off the alter and putting tables and chairs around the sanctuary. Wedding cake was served and each guest was given a cardboard box gift to take home. When we got home after eight, we found it was a box of sandwiches, which became our supper. Edward slept all the way home in the car for he was exhausted from running from table to table entertaining the wedding guests.

May 25, 1952

Today was a rather typical Sunday—preaching in the morning, elders meeting in the afternoon with another preaching service in the evening at Tondabayashi. That is Shigeko-san's town where we visited her last Thursday and found her confined to bed (lying on a *futon* on the floor) with peritonitis. Edward seemed a bit disturbed to see her in bed for he is used to her working around the house and playing with him.

Tomorrow morning we are going to an American circus in Nishinomiya with Pastor Hashimoto's family and a friend. I have to stop for a committee meeting in Osaka on the way back. It seems that a complete day off is becoming a rarity.

Driving is hazardous here. Last Wednesday I had an accident on a crowded street in the outskirts of Osaka. I was carefully watching a line of uniformed school children being led down the left side of the street when suddenly an elderly man ran out from a saloon door on my right. I screeched to a stop but not before my front tire had hit his foot a glancing blow. Several policeman appeared from nearby and we took him to the hospital for a checkup. Fortunately no bones were broken but I am sure it did hurt a lot.

Of course, I paid the hospital bill and I may pay for some lost days at "work." It seems his "work" is to gamble on bicycle races and he says he can't "run after the bicycles" if his foot hurts. I think I will pay for a week or so of "work" as a goodwill gesture. He appears to be quite poor and I certainly want to be as fair and generous with him as the situation warrants. There is enough bitterness toward the "rich Americans taking over" a defeated Japan without adding uncompensated injury to the insult.

June 2, 1952

Pastor Hashimoto went to visit his family home in Hyogo Prefecture and from there sent a telegram to our local church saying he is resigning. He contends the church people are putting too much emphasis on the new school and "neglecting evangelism." I believe Nakayama-sensei, the founder of the local school, is just as "evangelistic" as Pastor Hashimoto, but the elder which Nakayama-sensei brought in to be school principal is just as strong willed as Pastor Hashimoto and they frequently clash on church and school issues, so the real problem seems to be a personality conflict. Maybe Japanese church problems are not too different from American church troubles.

Last Saturday night our elder's meeting lasted until almost midnight trying to work out the conflict between Pastor Hashimoto and Elder Shinichi Ueda, the school principal. Sunday morning Hashimoto preached and conducted the communion service but the whole church was filled with gloom and doom. Ueda-sensei was the liturgist and made several mistakes—which is not like him. Yesterday afternoon a respected older pastor from Sakai city, Saito-sensei, was called in to help mediate the disagreements. His advice is for Hashimoto to stay on, which I happen to think is the right decision. In spite of their conflicts, Pastor Hashimoto and Principal Ueda need each other to get God's church going and the school work done. I am getting initiated into church and school difficulties rather rapidly.

June 9, 1952

Pastor Hashimoto still talks about resigning. I preached for him yesterday morning. The elders met after church for three hours and I listened as they struggled with the problem. Hashimoto has given three conditions for staying on: 1). A new church building be built before the proposed kindergarten; 2). The lady evangelist he works with be assigned to the preaching point at Tondabayashi (apparently there is a personality conflict there as well as with Principal Ueda and Lillian has clashed with her in some of the Sunday school teachers meetings, but Lillian usually gives in and patiently waits—and the teachers, including the lady evangelist, Kitano-sensei, finally come around to seeing that Lillian's ideas have merit and puts them into practice, but Hashimoto is less patient); and 3). Any elder who deserved it should be punished (who would do the punishing and how)?

This last request seemed strange to us but it is fitting with the Japanese mindset for they have the idea that the head of an institution (Principal Ueda) is like the father of a household who has the right to decide for his wife and children without consulting them: "Father knows best."

Another legitimate complaint is that Pastor Hashimoto and his family live in very cramped quarters. The former pastor, a member of the "outcast" group (formerly called "Eta," now called "Village People"), died in the manse during the war when Christians were suspected as spies by some non-Christian Japanese. Even some of the Christians turned against him in the poisonous atmosphere of the war, but his being an "outcast" made it all the worse. His wife became a mental case and was allowed to stay on in the manse.

This prevents Hashimoto and his family from using the manse, so they live in cramped rented quarters with only two rooms and a small kitchen. I think his family will eventually get to live in the manse and the elders will try to be more democratic but I am afraid he will not get more than that. The Evangelist, Kitano-sensei, has been at the church longer than Hashimoto and they would let him go before her. She is a native of Nagano and thus "one of them." There is to be an elders meeting Wednesday night with a full congregational meeting on Thursday night with Hashimoto present but with a neutral pastor to preside.

Oddly, two of the major complaints against the pastor who died during the war was that he let his wife hang out babies' diapers to dry in the back of the sanctuary on rainy days and that he built a toilet near the entrance of the church to prevent church members coming into his private home on Sundays to use his toilet. Supposedly he built the toilet "without their permission."

Lillian, who is due in September, was surprised when a lady gave her a seat on the train in Osaka last Wednesday. Men never think of it. Often we see a young couple on the train with the man seated and his girlfriend standing in front of him swinging on a strap to keep from falling. They chat as if it is the most natural thing in the world—as it is under their customs.

June 15, 1952

It is settled. Hashimoto will remain as pastor. He gave his reasons for wanting to resign and apologized for notifying the session by telegram. Principal Ueda gave a conciliatory speech (as much as his stern personality would allow) but the evangelist, Miss Kitano, refused to say anything.

I discovered that one reason she gives Pastor Hashimoto such a rough time is that she offered to marry him before he married his present wife and has never really forgiven him for turning him down. According to Hashimoto she came to him and said "God has told me that I should marry you." Hashimoto's response was "But God has not told me that." I hope things will calm down a bit now so we can get on with the much-needed church and school work.

Edward is full of mosquito bites and his face and body is raw in spots where he has scratched them. We put a net over his crib but he doesn't like it and pushes it off. We haven't been able to get window screens installed yet and we almost suffocate from the muggy heat when we close the windows. The concrete basement wall of our apartment serves as one bank of the sizable river that runs beneath our windows and mosquitos breed freely there as well as in the many flooded rice fields around us.

Today I preached at the distant town of Izumi-Sano, near my new preaching point at Kaizuka, where I go every Friday night. A man from Kaizuka was to meet us there, get in our car and guide us to the church. When we arrived he had four girls with him. All five of them crowded into the back of the car (meant to seat three) and we chugged along with the heavy load. Unfortunately my brakes began to give way and I had to proceed very slowly and carefully to the church.

A nearby garage fixed the brakes while I conducted the worship service. On the way back we ate a picnic lunch at a lovely seaside park with a white sandy beach which Edward loved. We hope to visit again. After getting home I had time to rest briefly before preaching again at Tondabayashi.

Friday night while I was at Kaizuka, the carpenter delivered a dish cabinet which we had ordered. This is the way Lillian reported it in a letter home: "At 9:30 P.M. the carpenter arrived with the cabinet. I was in a kimono planning to take a bath any minute. . . . It was a little embarrassing but we managed to get through the transaction; however, I didn't serve him tea! He can't understand a word of English and my Japanese is not up to much of a conversation so it was a little difficult, especially since any such business transaction becomes a social event after the business is settled. He lit up a cigarette after I paid him and tried to carry on but finally gave up when I just couldn't hold up my end of the conversation!"

June 22, 1952

On Thursday morning we went to Omi Hachiman to tour the famous Omi Brotherhood Christian Center with its school, churches and mentholatum factory established by the legendary evangelist Merril Vories Hitotsuyanagi who came to Japan as a YMCA worker and then taught English in the public schools until forced to stop by Buddhist priests who opposed his Christian work. His main income now is from his architectural firm and he is drawing up plans for our new missionary home in Nagano-cho.

We had six adults and one child in our small five-passenger "Americar." Again we had car trouble and arrived at noon, a couple hours late. After lunch we toured the school, church, sanitarium, YMCA, mentholatum factory and architectural offices. We now understand why this man has moved from being a persecuted outsider to become the most powerful influence in the whole area. He married a noble lady, daughter of a powerful daimyo, (whose name he adopted), became a Japanese citizen and remained in Japan during World War II.

At first he was persecuted but when the government decided they needed mentholatum for every soldier's medical kit, he was allowed to start his business up again and then allowed to operate fairly normally the rest of the war period—even his evangelistic church work was grudgingly permitted. His Christian buildings, including churches in nearby towns, are scattered over a wide area which increases their influence.

Merril's hair is white now but his complexion is ruddy and he talks with much energy, humor and enthusiasm. He has a Christian radio program and educational extension program which promote Bible classes throughout the main island of Japan, Honshu. He told us he expected to get the rights to produce Airwick in Japan as another business venture. All the people who work for him earn the same salary, with allowances for children and health care. All profits go into evangelistic efforts.

Edward is showing his rebellion at my being away so much. He was angry when I left early this morning and Lillian said he refused to use his potty but rather wet on the floor twice. When I got back at noon I helped Lillian get lunch started and then took Edward with me to the bank to try to make amends for being away so much—which is perhaps the most difficult part of my work.

Today my language teacher, Tamura-sensei invited me to attend a formal tea with her tea ceremony teacher. Twelve of us entered the tea house through an opening only large enough to crawl through, symbolizing our humility. Our group sat cozily around the *hibachi* with the kettle of boiling water in the small, straw mat room. The teacher went through an elaborate ceremony, admiring the ceramic bowls, with each of us handling them in turn, then putting hot water in a bowl and swishing the green powdered tea around in it with a wooden brush until it foams. Then each sips from the bowl, wipes it carefully with a cloth and passes it on to the next guest seated on the adjoining floor cushion with legs drawn up underneath them.

Over several hours this is repeated three times in addition to a Japanese breakfast which had been served earlier. The green tea is rich in caffeine (students use it to stay awake to study for exams). The honored guest—which I was—is expected to drink the most, so I was getting pretty tense, red faced and hyperactive by the end! It was becoming a bit difficult to maintain the quiet dignity required for such occasions, especially after sitting on legs that are numb after the first hour. Even so I did enjoy it and managed to complete the ceremony without embarrassing Tamura-sensei.

We survived our first flood, about two weeks ago. The water from the river washed against the basement wall of our house and entered on the Hayakawa side but did little damage to us as we have nothing in the basement. One night I slept with my clothes on expecting to have to evacuate our family at any time. The nearby bridge to town washed away and we now have to go almost a mile down river to a big car bridge to even get into town for shopping. This was part of a typhoon (Japanese *taifu*) which is a bit early for usually they come in August or September. Our neighbors blame the flood on a nearby luxury hotel which built a dam across the river resulting in the riverbanks becoming shallow because of the silting in behind the dam.

We were impressed by the many Christian friends who

came to check on us, many bringing gifts of food. Since about 20 church members showed up during the morning, Lillian made a big pot of coffee and served them cinnamon toast and cookies. Both train lines and automobile roads were washed out in several places around us. We survived the excitement and realized what good friends these people are to us. Our path out of the apartment is now so narrow we have to carry both Edward and his stroller in our arms.

July 21, 1952

The flood took out some town water pipes and yesterday the Hayakawas used up all the water in our mutual well so we have had to carry water home from a neighbor's house where there is water gushing out from between rocks on the steep hillside. This, of course, hast to be boiled before we can drink it. Lillian and our new helper, Setsuko-san, tried doing our laundry in the river but we know it is polluted and the clothing had black spots all over it.

Most of our neighbors think nothing of washing in the river and seldom bother to boil water for safety purposes. They think we are awfully fussy about our laundry and drinking water but our experience with intestinal parasites reminds us that the water could contain even greater dangers, with so many people living all along the river. Most laundry is done in cold water here. The worst part is that we have a lot of laundry to do this week as we go to Tokyo next week on vacation and to prepare for the birth of our second child. From our window we can see several naked little boys swimming in the polluted river. A few of the older ones wear G-strings but most of them don't bother. I wonder when Edward gets older if he will want to join the skinny-dipping crowd.

He is in rather an unhappy state right now. Something he ate plus the heat caused him to break out all over and we have to give him soda baths every couple of hours. For two days he had diarrhea but that is better now. It may be tomatoes he is allergic to, but he does look a sight and we are trying to watch his diet carefully. Since his room is so hot we have been putting him to bed an hour later, at eight, because it is cooler. It gradually cools off here beside the river so the latter part of the night is more comfortable. He sleeps fairly well so must not be too sick.

Our life is never dull. This week we had an earthquake—like the flood it was the biggest that has ever been known in this area. We seem to be hitting all the big events in Nagano-cho. It woke us up about midnight and the bed got a good shaking for about ten minutes. Kyoto had it even worse than we did, but many of the casualties were caused by people leaping out of second story windows. As usual panic precipitated more damage than the actual event. Lillian wondered what we should do in case one of us died in Japan. It seemed logical to assume we would be cremated just as the Japanese are for lack of burial space.

A factory siren had started following the shaking and I thought this meant "prepare for more!" I lay awake for about an hour but Lillian went right back to sleep—either she is more resigned to these things than I am, or else she is just too worn out to stay awake. Later she said, "When the moment comes for us to go to our heavenly home we probably won't have much time to think of it in advance anyway."

With the heavy rains and steep hills here mud slides are another cause of damage and death. The police borrowed our car on Saturday and called again today to borrow it. Dr. Sawada warned us not to let them have it as they would want it all the time. Fortunately I could say no today because we have to have some work done on it. Maybe they will get out of the habit while we are away for summer vacation.

August 4, 1952—Tokyo

We are renting the Buckley's home while they are on vacation from their YMCA work. This city living is simply luxurious. We cook with gas, have city water and electricity every day and rattle around in the largest house we've ever lived in.

Edward is so excited by the house and the new helper, Keiko-san, he has given up sleeping through the night. Last night at three I heard a voice beside my bed saying "water" and there he was. He tries on everyone's shoes in the *genkan* (entrance) and doesn't understand why he can't walk through the house in them, including the *tatami* rooms. Every morning he is raring to go at five. We may have to go to bed at seven when he does to catch up on our sleep.

Keiko-san is a kindergarten teacher who is on her summer vacation. Being a Christian, she very kindly offered to help us out. Lillian's energy is sapped by the pregnancy and the heat and she could not get along without help here. Just cleaning this huge house is a big job. There are no refrigerators or ice boxes here so we try to keep cool by buying ice and keeping it in a plastic bucket. Even with food placed on the ice we can keep very little for long and have to shop for perishables every day, just like Japanese housewives do. Fortunately local markets are nearby in every community, even small villages.

August 13, 1952

Tomorrow I have to go back to Nagano-cho for some urgent church work. The extra rent, city expenses and travel make our budget pretty tight this month but we will manage, I believe, but we spent an hour this morning trying to work out a new budget.

Lillian has anemia which requires a daily injection at the hospital or at home. I am learning to give them to her and Mr. Buckley can give her one tomorrow. Keiko-san, or someone else, will have to help her until I can return on the 25th. A Japanese lady who is married to a YMCA executive lives nearby and may take care of the shots, although she seems a little nervous about it.

We have just visited the Fox family who live near an army base and enjoyed not only the fellowship but also the exotic American treats of hot dogs and fresh corn on the cob. Japanese corn in the local markets is usually too hard to eat. While at the Fox's we all recorded a message on tape to send to our folks back home. This is something new for us, but a great idea, so much more personal than a letter.

Saturday Tusjino-sensei of Seikyo Gakuen School in Nagano-cho visited us and we all went to the Ueno Zoo in Tokyo. All went fine until Lillian got too hot and tired and passed out in my arms. Fortunately, they had a room with a small cot in it (this must be a common occurrence here) and after resting a while Lillian was able to come home on the local train. She wanted to see the zoo but walking around in the heat was a bit too much. Aromatics which she carries with her revived her in a hurry. We then went to an air-conditioned movie while Tsujino-sensei finished seeing the zoo. He is taking a summer course at a local Christian university and will probably visit us every weekend.

Aug. 18, 1952—Nara-ken
Today is my birthday but it is just another day of evangelistic caravan work with local pastors and seminary students in the rural areas of Nara-ken (Prefecture). We visit towns and villages without churches and show Christian slides, put on puppet shows about Bible stories, use *Kamishibai* (stories illustrated by pictures on large cardboard squares), preach and have fellowship with as many people as we can. Then we stay overnight in the homes of Christian friends, eating too much and sleeping too little.

Aug. 19, 1952—Inasa-mura, Nara-ken
Today I sent the following message to Lillian: "The Lord blessed me on my birthday by allowing us to get to our next stop without the usual flat tire. We left Umami this morning and have just arrived in a beautiful spot in the mountains called Inasa. The farmer in whose house we will spend the night is wealthy in Japanese terms. He has two milk cows and two sheep. You would never believe a car could get into the roads we came over to get here, but once here it is really lovely. Louie Grier is away so I am driving his car and it is worse than ours for flats and getting overheated. . . . See you Saturday night if all goes well."

Aug. 24, 1952—Tokyo

When Shigeko-san and I arrived last night we learned that Lillian and Edward had survived a fire on the 19th. Lillian described it thus in a letter to her parents in Baltimore: "Last night we had a fire in our home here. Fortunately only the *ofuro* room (bathroom) was damaged and Mrs. Hamada, the owner of the house, has assumed full responsibility for the incident. She was here yesterday to check up on everything and prepared the *ofuro* for us in the afternoon.

"Keiko-san had the day off and when she came home at seven I told her she could take a bath. A few minutes later she went into the bathroom and saw smoke coming out of the walls. She called me and started throwing water on the walls. Then I told her to call the neighbors and also telephone a nearby fire station. Mr. Kimoto, who works at the Y with Mr. Buckley, came too and sent Edward and me over to his house.

"We learned later that the firemen came and broke in the roof, quickly extinguishing the fire. We were soon able to return and Edward slept soundly while the police took pictures right and left and interviewed Mrs. Hamada, Keiko-san and Mr. Kimoto. There seems to have been something wrong with the gas pipes. . . . People are still swarming all over the place and Edward is awake and enjoying it thoroughly."

Aug. 24, 1952

Edward seems to get a "daddy complex" quite often, probably because I am away so much. I took care of him today while Lillian and Shigeko-san went to a church meeting and he refused to take his usual afternoon nap, crying for about two hours before finally falling into an exhausted sleep. I wish I didn't have to leave him so often but the work requires it. Lillian is now having to take anemia shots about twice a week. While I was away Mrs. Kimoto gave the shots with what Lillian called "fear and trembling."

At dinner tonight we celebrated my birthday as a family a few days late. With our new baby due soon Lillian is huge. When I made a wish before blowing out the birthday candles, she said, "You better not wish for twins."

Sept. 2, 1952

When I got back from the fellowship conference at Karuizawa and a visit to check on the cabin we are buying at Lake Nojiri, I told Lillian of the wonderful corn on the cob and the blueberries available at Nojiri. She was quite jealous as the corn in the local markets is allowed to get hard because the Japanese eat it like peanuts. If the baby does not come soon we will have to move in with the Oltmans to continue waiting as the Buckleys need this house in a few days. Lillian is taking the unsettled life very well but is quite uncomfortable with the hot, sticky weather here. However, the city luxuries available in Tokyo such as the American drug store with its banana splits makes up for it.

Sept. 7, 1952

We visited the Nikkatsu Building and found that the fancy hotel which occupies the top three floors has double rooms for only $12 a night. The whole building is air-conditioned, unusual here. In a large coffee shop in the basement they even have chocolate and strawberry ice cream (when usually we can find vanilla only). Fancy shops sell jewelry, fur coats and luxury items at fantastically high prices. After seeing a movie we returned for some soft ice cream and found it was flavored with banana, an unheard of luxury. If we don't return to the small town of Nagano-cho soon we will be too spoiled to "rough it" there anymore. We are going to the Tokyo Union Church this afternoon and stay for dinner there. One of my friends is preaching. Shigeko-san went this morning.

Sept. 19, 1952

Today Wayland Davis, a sergeant in the army who is married to our cousin Dot, came to Tokyo on "R & R" and visited us. I took him out to dinner and when I got back to the Oltmans, I discovered Lillian's bag of water had broken suddenly and Mrs. Oltman had rushed her to the hospital in a taxi. I followed immediately and found Lillian in labor but doing well.

It was an easy birth compared to Edward's although Lillian always seems to lose a lot of blood. She is not a hemophiliac but has always been much more of a "free bleeder" than most people which is one of the reasons we came to Tokyo to be near a Christian hospital—the Seventh Day Adventist Hospital *(Eisei Byoin)* at Ogikubo. Lillian is adjusting well to the fact that the hospital will serve only a vegetarian diet—no meat and postum in place of coffee. I tried the food and liked it. They are certainly taking good care of Lillian and our new baby daughter, Mary Lillian, who is cute as can be.

Sept. 21, 1952

Lillian is fine but the second day after birth Mary started turning yellow with jaundice and refused to eat. The doctors thought it was physiological jaundice which would clear up in a few days; however, at my insistence, they checked our blood and found that it is an Rh factor blood problem. I am Rh positive and Lillian is negative and Mary's blood is positive making it vulnerable to Lillian's antibodies left in Mary's system at birth. If Mary's jaundice and appetite don't improve she may have to receive a Rh negative blood transfusion which would cut down the antibody destruction of her red blood cell count and hemoglobin until the antibodies gradually flush out of her system letting her own blood stay healthy.

Sept. 29, 1952

Mary's red blood count and hemoglobin slowly went downward each day so the hospital began a search for Rh negative blood. Not a single nurse or doctor in the hospital had it nor could we find a missionary or Japanese friend with it. It seems that while 17 people out of 100 in the U.S. have negative type blood only 1 in 100 among Japanese people do.

The "Rh" comes from the Rhesus monkey which always has positive blood. I joked with Lillian that this probably means I am more closely related to the monkeys than she is.

Our frantic search for Rh negative blood finally ended when we found the U.S. Army Blood Bank had some available. So exactly one week after birth Mary had a complete blood transfusion. The doctor called it "drain, flush and refill," a slow process which took three hours while Lillian and I waited nervously to see how it would come out.

The change was amazing. Almost like a miracle, Mary's jaundice began to clear up immediately and she was eager to nurse again. I wonder if she will later refer to it as the complete "oil change" she had at the tender age of a week. That is certainly one good deed the army did for us in Japan.

The nurses call Mary "Momo-chan" (peach child) as she started life with yellow skin. Lillian had been doing well but right after Mary's blood problem was solved Lillian started her free bleeding bad habit again. With more shots for anemia and an increase of her thyroid medication she is feeling better but cannot leave the hospital to go to the Oltmans yet.

Oct. 5, 1952

Lillian finally got back to the Oltman's home last Friday. If all goes well we can go back to Nagano next Friday. Living out of a suitcase in other people's homes has not been easy. Although our Nagano-cho home is simple we will be happy to get back, but we can't rush it because of Lillian's bleeding tendency. God's grace which has "brought us safe thus far" will certainly "lead us home."

Oct. 14, 1952—Osaka and Nagano

Last week I had one of the scariest nights of my life. We arrived safely in Osaka from Tokyo at five in pouring rain and went by taxi to the missionary home on the campus of Osaka Jo Gajuin where Liba and Ed Daub are living temporarily. All went well until we went to bed about ten when Lillian started passing large clots of blood followed by fresh blood. The Daubs were asleep, and couldn't help us anyway, and I didn't know a single doctor or hospital in Osaka.

With frantic applications of ice bags to her womb area

Lillian finally stopped bleeding, but she never moved from the living room couch all night. I kept busy filling the ice bag and emptying the bedpan for her. We waited two more days before attempting the short trip to Nagano-cho by train since Lillian would probably start bleeding again if we jolted over the rough roads by car.

Back at Nagano she went to bed immediately with some slight bleeding and has stayed upstairs in bed ever since, getting up only to nurse Mary and eat her own meals which we take up to her. Shigeko-san has graciously stayed overnight to help get meals and clean up. With a full schedule of work, I could not manage without her help.

This morning I taught for four hours at Seikyo Gakuen School and entertained guests coming to see the new baby all afternoon. No wonder all of us are struggling to overcome bad colds. Fortunately a Japanese lady doctor has agreed to visit Lillian and Mary here at home until Lillian is able to get out again. A new footbridge to replace the one that washed out was a welcome sight when we returned. I don't think Lillian would have survived the mile walk around to the big car bridge we had to use before. We have to carry water in from a well about a block away and have no money to replace the system as our expensive summer has left us really broke.

Oct. 20, 1952

Edward's second birthday party last Saturday was, for him, a big event. Not only did the entire Hashimoto family come but a lady and her daughter who dropped by to bring a present for one-month-old Mary stayed to celebrate Edward becoming two years old. Edward showed off by speaking almost entirely in Japanese.

We laugh to think what mistaken preconceptions we had about that. We had assumed Japanese would be a problem and English easy for him. It is just the reverse. He spends so much time with Japanese helpers and children that his English gives way to Japanese. We made the mistake of deliberately speaking in Japanese to him, assuming that would be difficult for him to learn. Now we have to revise our plan and speak English to him for that is his problem. It is a sign of our cultural arrogance to assume that since he is American by birth English would be easy for him and Japanese difficult. Another lesson in humility.

Oct. 26, 1952

Our septic tank overflowed and in locating where it is stopped up, I discovered that the whole system is nothing more than a large holding tank with an over-flow pipe directly into the river. It took me almost two days to clean out the entire system. We feel that we have been misled by the owner who promised us a "flush toilet, piped in water and hot bath system." We actually have none of these at the moment and, although he swears that the system is sanitary and that it is legal to drain into the river, the owner is probably liable to prosecution for building a system that must pollute the river. Our plans to build our own home becomes ever more an imperative.

Nov. 3, 1952

At the tender age of a month Mary was baptized yesterday by Pastor Hashimoto. He almost drowned her by pouring three large handfuls of water over her head—one for the Father, one for the Son and one for the Holy Spirit. He is accustomed to baptizing adults but this was his first infant baptism. His wife is a former Baptist, so none of their children were baptized as infants. Other children in the church are only dedicated since infant baptism seems to upset Mrs. Hashimoto. I admire Pastor Hashimoto for agreeing to baptize Mary over his wife's objections. Since Mary is a "foreigner" I think Mrs. Hashimoto was willing to relax her standards a bit in this case. At least she still seems to be friendly toward us.

Since Mary's baptism fell on the regular first Sunday communion day—with congratulations and pictures following—we decided to eat out since it was too late to get dinner at home. We drove to nearby Tondabayashi and ate *udon* (noodles), *domburi* (rice with meat and vegetables on top), fruit, tea and doughnuts all for the total cost of 75¢ for two adults and one child. The small-town restaurant was rather dirty but the food was clean and tasty. Think how much money we could save if we ate Japanese food all the time! Unfortunately the heavy emphasis on rice would probably make us gain quite a bit of weight.

Shigeko-san called in sick again today. Apparently her peritonitis is a chronic condition. We gave her a week off soon after Mary was born and she has missed many days in the past two months. Fortunately she always seems to get better eventually. In the meantime we have been getting a middle-aged widow, Matsuda-san, from the Nagano church to help in Shigeko-san's place. She has three sons and one daughter.

Her husband was a sergeant in the Japanese Army in Manchuria and they were quite wealthy there, owning several houses which they rented out. Of course they lost everything when the army was defeated. Matsuda-san returned to Japan with a sick husband—who soon died—and four children to care for. Her strong faith and healthy, small body enabled her to care for them by taking jobs wherever she could—cleaning houses, washing clothes or doing domestic chores. When I had to clean out the septic tank she worked beside me without a word of complaint about the dirty, smelly job.

She is also a great church school teacher and uses most of her days off to teach young children in the surrounding villages, all on her own initiative. Her oldest son told me she speaks in tongues at home but she has never done so at church. She always attends our Thursday night prayer meetings and prays deep, meaningful prayers in a calm, quiet voice. It is obvious her profound faith in God's love and mercy has enabled her to overcome her trials and keep her sanity when a lesser person would have broken under the strain. Now she is trying to get a job as a cook and house-keeper for a public nursery school which would give her more income and security than she now has. She is a real model of Christian faith and love in action.

Today is "Culture Day" and when I went to Tondabayashi this morning to get our dry cleaning and arrange for some car repairs I saw an interesting art exhibit which I took Lillian to see this afternoon. Here is Lillian's written account: "When we had finished looking at the pictures and flowers and other works of art, Funeuchi-san suggested we have tea. Dressed in her gay kimono and Western hairdo she took me to an adjoining building where ceremonial tea was being served.

We had to take off our coats and shoes and I felt out of place in my sweater and skirt. I sat on my knees in true Japanese style even though they kept insisting I sit some other way if I preferred. They told me what to do. Cake and candy were served first and we took it off the plate and put it on a paper napkin in front of us on the rug on which we kneeled. Then the plate was removed, refilled and another was served. All the time a girl with a very serious expression was preparing the green tea beside me. It is all very formal but my presence added a lighter touch to the whole ceremony since as a foreigner I did not understand the system.

The girl preparing the tea never smiled once during the ceremony. When she had finished, after bowing she placed a large bowl with a little green tea in it before me. I was told to take the bowl and turn it one quarter of a turn and then drink all the tea, turn it back one quarter of a turn (marked by design) and place it in front of her again, where it was taken and refilled for the next person. I don't like the tea and many of the Japanese don't either. It is a thick green tea and has rather a bitter taste. The ceremony to prepare it is very elaborate and girls study for a long time to learn it exactly."

Nov. 17, 1952

Plans for building our own home in Nagano are making some progress although bureaucratic wheels turn slowly here. The land we are buying for $400 has to be formally changed from "farm land" to "residential land." Today I went with my request to the town committee carrying the customary gift, a basket of fruit, which is called a polite gift—but feels like a bribe to me. The missionary architect Merril Vories Hitotsu-yanagi has come up with a plan for a two-story house of four bedrooms which will cost about $8,500 to build. It sounds like a lot to us, but it is to be made of good materials and suitable to handle a family our size (or larger).

The Interboard Committee working with us has approved the plans. The living-dining area is separated by sliding wooden doors so we can have church meetings for up to 20 people there. The second story is designed to have the children well away from evening meetings on the first floor so they can sleep without being disturbed too much. We hope to start building soon.

We are under a lot of stress living in cramped Japanese quarters. Because of the dampness and proximity to the river Lillian has had asthma attacks and all four of us seem to have constant colds. The new house should help alleviate some of this for I am convinced our health requires better living conditions. Mary is beginning to sleep through her 2 A.M. feeding now so we are getting a little more rest with our two-month old baby growing up.

Rev. Kiyoshi Tanimoto has been our famous house guest this week. He was exposed to the atomic radiation when Hiroshima was bombed and is now making the rounds to get funds and other support for radiation victims. He is a Methodist minister from Hiroshima who became famous in America through an article written by Norman Cousins in the *Saturday Review of Literature* and has made two trips to America since the war to promote the Hiroshima Peace Center Foundation Inc. Many noted Americans have backed him and the World Peace Foundation which recently met in Hiroshima.

He speaks perfect English having studied at Emory Seminary in Atlanta before the war and we became amazingly well acquainted in the short time he spent with us sleeping on our studio couch in the living room. He wears false teeth which bother him, has four children who wake them three or four times every night and dreads getting shots for anything!

Nov. 23, 1952

This morning the new bride and groom came to say thank you to us for attending their wedding. Mrs. Hayakawa's brother married the sister of one of our kindergarten teachers in an arranged marriage but they seem to be happy together. Since they will be new neighbors, living in two rooms with the Hayakawa's, they followed Japanese custom in bringing us a gift and saying *"doozo yoroshiku"* (please be friendly).

At the wedding the bride wore a beautiful kimono, had her hair up in a formal pompadour, wore elegant ladies sandals and had her face white with makeup (symbolizing feminine beauty and purity, I think). We feel a little sorry for her since she will be under the control of Mrs. Hayakawa, the "lady of the house," who can be rather domineering at times.

They said they were taking a trip to Osaka. Lillian later repeated the word "Osaka" and it came out "Osaki" (rice wine). The groom said *"dame desu"* (that's bad) which must mean he doesn't drink (unlike Mr. Hayakawa who imbibes freely and who told me that when coming home late at night after drinking with friends, he sometimes goes to sleep on the train and rides past his stop and then has to come back from the next town). After leaving their gift of delicious little cakes, the couple left to call on other neighbors. For their sake we hope they can have their own home soon.

Dec. 8, 1952

After many months without running water—ever since the pipes were destroyed when the nearby river bridge washed away—we now have new pipes in. Seeing the welcome water gush out, Lillian said she wanted to declare a holiday and just stand there turning the water on and off all day.

Our little house was really crowded on Tuesday. I was talking with the architect and several contractors about plans for our new house in one room while Lillian was entertaining guests in an adjoining room with only paper sliding doors separating us. Since noise travels easily through a paper door it was hard to keep the conversations separated. We will really be glad when our new house is built. Life and work will be a lot easier to handle.

Pastor Hashimoto came to plan Christmas meetings with me and I was amazed to find we have about 20 meetings to conduct in approximately ten days, before and after Christmas. Even secular schools, and some non-Christian families, celebrate Christmas with a party featuring a "Christmas Decoration Cake" along with other snacks and drinks. Every department store, and many private shops, also observe the season in a highly commercialized style.

Dec. 14, 1952

Last night was the annual missionaries Christmas party in Osaka. It started in the late afternoon with children's programs, dinner, business meeting, carol singing, instrumental numbers, solos and finally ended with a movie (which turned out to be pretty dull), so we left early, took the Daubs home in our car and finally arrived home after ten. It was midnight before we got the children tucked in and fell exhausted into bed ourselves. It was good to get together and enjoy an American prepared meal. There was a slight problem with the jello salad and the potatoes but it all turned out fine in the end. Edward and Mary were so excited they could hardly eat, which may have been good since little Philip Daub ate too much and lost his dinner in our car on the way home. Edward's present from under the tree was a set of boxes that fit into each other and Mary got an inflatable toy Bambi.

Since the big celebration for Japanese people is New Year's, it works well for Shigeko-san to help us through Christmas and then take her holiday and help her mother get ready for their New Year's celebration. Shigeko-san is a good, steady worker from the time she comes in the morning until six in the evening.

We pay her a little better than the going rate and supplement her salary with nice gifts on occasion, but it still seems awfully small compared to American rates—her ¥1,000 per week amounts to only a little over three dollars. She will also stay overnight whenever we need her to babysit. I know she would like to marry again, but since her first marriage was annulled and with her chronic peritonitis, there are obstacles to be overcome.

Louis Grier has a set of puppets which we use on our evangelistic caravans and we invited him to bring them for some of our Christmas programs. Using puppets to tell the Christmas story is quite effective with our kindergarten children—and even older children and adults. Japanese *bunraku* puppets are world-famous which may account for why the Japanese like puppets so much. I am learning to help with the puppets, and today Lillian and I are practicing a piano and guitar duet for the annual school festival.

Dec. 29, 1952

Carolers from the church arrived at six Christmas morning and we served them cocoa, cookies and nuts. Fortunately we already had the kerosene stove going to chase away the 40° cold air that greets us each morning now.

Although our house seems small and inconvenient it is better than the one adjoining the church building where the pastor's family live. As you enter their house you come into a small room, about six by nine. Beyond paper sliding doors is their one main room which is a little larger. All the floors are straw mats except for a small corner of the main room which is wood and upon which sits a one-burner kerosene stove which they have just bought to cook with. There is also a *hibachi* with another large ceramic jar filled with charcoal which is used both for heating and cooking. They use grates over these open fires and set pans on top of the grate.

There is no water in the house so it must be carried from the church yard quite a distance away. The main room contains a cabinet with doors from the floor to ceiling which is used to store dishes and food. One corner of the room is curtained off to hide their clothing and *futon* which is spread on the floor mats every night and taken up every morning, and occasionally hung outside to air. Above the curtained off area is a shelf where there are stacks of boxes containing other family belongings. They have put two of the kindergarten benches together to make a bed for their little girl.

They really need a house much more than we do and I certainly hope it will be possible for them to get one soon. However, the church is busy raising money to improve the kindergarten so it will probably be a long time. If the pastor got money for a house he would probably use it for the kindergarten, anyway, as they always seem to put the church and kindergarten needs first before personal needs.

It makes us feel quite guilty to be planning such a lovely home, but the church people seem to be even more excited about it than we are. They know it will be paid for by the mission board and will be used for church meetings as well as for our home. Incidentally, Mrs. Hashimoto, the pastor's wife, was thrilled to get to live in our small Japanese home when we were away for a month for vacation. Her favorite was our washing machine, which she had never seen before— much less gotten to use, to wash her clothing. Recently three women from the Tomioka church dropped by for a visit and discreetly let it be known they would like to see a demonstration of our washing machine.

Although funding for our new house is delayed we will probably start building in March as most of the plans are completed with the contractors ready to go anytime the funds come. It will be on the other side of Stone River (Ishi-kawa) where the main part of the town of Nagano is located. This will be a great advantage as the small walking bridge we use is often washed out by floods and we have to go the long way around to a car bridge, which takes us through the red light district of Nagano-cho.

Recently a beautiful young woman and her servant came by with a large denomination German mark note asking me how much it is worth. I knew they were from the red light district and suspected this German money was for services rendered to a German tourist. They said the local bank would not give them an immediate evaluation and they were in a hurry to know how much this was worth.

I gave them an educated guess but I could not help praying that some of these women will come to know the liberating good news of God's love in Jesus Christ. They know we are missionaries and are always very careful to speak in a friendly fashion when we go by, making a big fuss over Edward and Mary. Without Christ, what hope have they for the future when they can no longer sell their physical charms?

Jan. 2, 1953

Yesterday was the big New Year's celebration for our landlord's family and they invited us to an early morning feast of New Year's goodies that included red colored rice, fancy fish of several types, chicken teriyaki, candied beans and an endless number of side dishes—all washed down by generous servings of rice wine which was served in a kind of saucer. Lillian didn't even want to try it, so Mrs. Hayakawa said, "Just put it up to your lips and pretend to drink so you can fulfill the New Year's obligation and still not get tipsy."

Jan. 19, 1953

Last Thursday was a Japanese national holiday when all 20-year-olds are recognized as adults. It is traditional in Japan to count one's age from January 1 rather than from your actual birthday so a baby born on New Year's Eve would be counted as a year old the next day. Consequently many Japanese people get confused as to what their exact age is.

It is also the custom to count years according to the era name given to the ruling emperor. For example 1953 means *"Showa 28"* for the 28th year of the rule of Emperor Hirohito. Since emperors often begin a new era in the middle of a calendar year this makes it hard to pin down historical dates in an exact manner. For that reason some Japanese historians use both the Japanese era name and the Western calendar to record dates.

Jan. 26, 1953

Our two year old Edward insists on helping to "clean house" now which for him means moving his toys from one spot to another—be it from the floor to the toy box or from the box to the couch. A recent favorite trick is to put his small toys in a pan and put them in the oven to "bake." He handles the pan very carefully with a potholder in one hand but sometimes forgets and grabs the other side of the pan with his bare hand. He also is beginning to join in the singing at Sunday school but often improvises his own words and notes to the songs.

Last Sunday I preached at Tomioka in the morning and went to Kaizuka in the afternoon for a planning meeting in addition to the regular worship. They now have eleven members, with several more attending meetings and want to start looking for land upon which to build a church building. None of them have much money but we are starting to build up a small fund and have the possibility of making a down payment on a lot and paying the rest gradually. Several small groups we are working with are trying to do the same thing, including Tondabayashi and Hatsushiba, so our tithe is stretched pretty thin trying to help all of them. We are beginning to wonder if we can afford the luxury of even a used car as it uses up so much of our "work funds" for gasoline and repairs. Even though we use the car for church business and summer evangelistic caravans would be impossible without it, still it is difficult to decide.

Television has just come to our town of Nagano, picking up at least one station in Osaka but we know only one person who has a set—a friend of ours who owns and operates the local radio shop and sells small appliances.

Our family seems very vulnerable to colds. Today I spent most of my regular day off in bed trying to recuperate from my current one. With our church work increasing and two small children to care for both Lillian and I push too hard—which may be one reason we get so many colds. Of course most of the public places we visit, including some church services, have no heat even when the temperature is hovering just above freezing on winter days. Fortunately we have Shigeko-san to assist with cooking, cleaning and child care and our friends are understanding when we get sick and have to take a day off now and then.

Feb. 2, 1953

Word just came from Mr. Hannaford that $8,500 has been appropriated for our new house. If we begin building now we should be able to move in by September, maybe earlier. It will be wonderful to get more living space. After our frequent colds were followed by eye infections, we are now careful to wash our hands thoroughly each time we return home. On the doctor's advice I am also gargling each time I come back from visiting patients at the local T.B. hospital. War time hardships reduced the resistance of the Japanese people so infection is all around us. We buy oranges by the crate to keep doused in vitamin C. Fortunately citrus fruits are cheap here. You can't say that for beef which is at least three times more expensive here than in the States.

The warm clothing we just received from Mother Cassel is truly appreciated. Last Sunday I spoke and visited several churches in the Kishiwada, Kaizuka and Izumi-Sano areas— none of which were heated. With no heater in the car there was no place to warm up from early morning to late at night except for a couple times when I warmed my hands over a charcoal *hibachi* while visiting in homes.

I agree with the Quaker teacher of the Crown Prince, Miss Grace Vining, who wrote in her book, *Windows For The Crown Prince*, that the Japanese theory that if you get your hands warm the whole body will be warm is defective. Even though I have constantly experienced that "cold hands, warm heart" is certainly true of the many fine Christian people here. They welcome me with warm hearts and open arms—and they don't have a heated living room to return to as I do. A young man, one of my first baptisms from Kaizuka who was formerly a Communist, swears he got T.B. from going from the hot public bath back home through the cold night air and then sleeping in an unheated room. Maybe he is right.

Feb. 8, 1953

Today we heard on the radio that the world-renowned missionary, E. Stanley Jones, will speak in Yokohama tomorrow. We are rather excited that this notable person will be sitting at our dinner table next Monday! I am going into Osaka and get him in the car so he can speak to the school and any of the general public who will come on Monday morning to his service. After this we will serve him, interpreter and musician dinner here. Lillian says sooner or later it seems everyone comes to Nagano, but she never dreamed E. Stanley Jones would number in that group. She is determined not to forget to have him sign our guest book. She says she is determined not to forget this time.

This past week we had two Japanese evangelists who are speaking in our area as our guests off and on for three days. Ishijima-sensei enjoys children and had a great time with Edward and Morono-sensei delighted him playing Japanese children's songs on our portable organ. We thoroughly enjoyed their witness and our Christian fellowship together.

The school just got a new wire voice recorder and one of the men recorded my sermon and prayer this morning. Lillian said my Japanese sermon sounded O.K. but she really liked the prayer in Japanese better as it sounded more "human." In the midst of her busy schedule Lillian has started studying Japanese again, fortunately her teacher, Reiko Tamura is very understanding when a class has to be postponed.

We are grateful to hear that we now have one more supporting church and over $200 in contributions toward building a new church in Tondabayashi.

Feb. 16, 1953

E. Stanley Jones gave a wonderful evangelistic message about the love of God for all people using good illustrations from his experience in India. At dinner today we learned he is a diabetic. Unfortunately Lillian had glazed the carrots and he couldn't eat those but he seemed to enjoy the oyster casserole, baked potatoes, celery and fruit. Being from Baltimore, as Lillian is, Dr. Jones especially likes seafood. He thanked us for the "Chesapeake" oysters.

Dr. Jones' Japanese musician has a three-day-old son he hasn't seen yet—a steep sacrifice to make. After dinner Dr. Jones took a nap in our upstairs bedroom while I showed slides to the others. The interpreter went to sleep in Lillian's boudoir chair watching the slides. Their schedule is so heavy they sleep whenever they get a chance.

Lillian had peanuts and a box of candy for them to eat after dinner. Dr. Jones grabbed a handful of peanuts on the way out, but his interpreter held his hand over the box of candy so he wouldn't take any of that. He showed me the litmus paper he used daily to test his urine for excess sugar.

Dr. Jones enjoyed using my new invention—putting rubber slippers inside heavy socks to wear inside when shoes must be taken off. I hope it kept him from catching a cold. It is much warmer than the four pairs of socks I used to wear.

We publicized the meeting by putting a large sign on the back of my car and driving slowly through the surrounding towns shouting the news through a megaphone from the car window and giving out printed leaflets everywhere.

About 175 turned out for the Monday morning service— which is a good turnout since most people must be at work. The school students were happy to miss classes to hear him speak and all told some 79 asked to learn more about Christianity and some even requested to be baptized with another 56 who signed cards saying they wanted to become better Christians. Pastor Hashimoto and I will follow up on all of these. He also has an inquirer's class every Tuesday evening.

This has been a busy week. Wednesday night we went to a missionary Valentine's party in Osaka. Thursday I went to prayer meeting and stayed late to help correct 10,000 handbills for Dr. Jones' meeting because the printer made an error so it had Sunday instead of Monday on them. Friday I worked in

Kaizuka all day. Saturday we invited three newlywed couples to our home for a Valentine's day dinner and evening of games. Sunday we publicized Dr. Jones' meeting, driving everywhere all day except for preaching time morning and evening for me. Four people from Kaizuka arrived for supper Sunday night. Then early Monday I picked up Dr. Jones and his group in Osaka and took them back late in the afternoon.

When the three couples came to play Valentine's games Shigeko-san took two-year-old Edward as her "husband" partner in the games. She is always saying he is like a little husband, the way he orders her around!

Feb. 23, 1953

Today we signed the contract for our new house with the architect plus three others from the contractor's office who did what was needed to get the building started. We staked out the actual measurements of the house and yard, including a combined storage and garage room at the back of the lot.

We have snow on the ground and Saturday I took Edward out to build a snowman. When we had finished it Edward went up to the snowman and said *"Konnichi wa"* (Hello!). At two he is learning proper Japanese social amenities.

March 3, 1953

This was a busy week: We got off our form letter to supporting churches and friends. Our mailman informed us the materials of our new house are already stacked up on the lot (it is the talk of the town for it is the first Western-style house to be built here). I let Mary fall off a table while bathing and dressing her (no damage). We had lunch at the home of our newlywed language teacher and then visited an Australian lady married to a Japanese man and learned of their international romance and five children. They never expected to live in Japan but got stuck here because of the war and his business (which has an office in Australia where they met). Two of their children are married and they have grandchildren. She speaks very poor Japanese, because she never studied it but just picked it up from what she heard around her. Having few opportunities to speak English she talked our ears off for more than an hour. Lillian says she understands this need to speak English very well. We hope to get this lady active in our Tomioka church and she shows some interest.

March 11, 1953

The new Osaka Hotel cooperated nicely in planning a surprise birthday party for Lillian on the ninth. I bought flowers for the table and the hotel dining room cooked a beautiful cake with "Happy Birthday, Lillian" on it. However, I had to provide the candles as they didn't have small ones available. The Western dinner was delicious. Since they are used to serving U.S. Army personnel, they know how to cook Western food well. Before leaving home we had birthday lunch. I couldn't find a birthday cake in Nagano so improvised with a round jelly roll with candles on it which amused Lillian a great deal. The hotel served us soup, a fish course, veal cutlet, spaghetti and a vegetable, an apple salad, roll and butter, coffee, ice cream and cake. The waitress put the leftover birthday cake in a box for us along with the red carnations and white daisies I had bought for the table. We concluded the celebration with a movie, *The Parade Case*.

The foundation of our new house is almost completed and we go almost every day to see how the building is progressing. Last Friday four young men came by to look at the site and then asked us to pose for a photo. While they were doing that three red fire engines drove up and stopped. We were surprised as there is nothing but the foundation which can't burn. The fire fighters said they were practicing to see if their fire trucks could get into the lot through the narrow roads. We were glad they made it as we may need them in the future, but were surprised to hear they wanted us to build a large water tank as well. Since the water pressure is so low on this hill we have to have a fairly large water tank in the attic anyway so we agreed to compromise with that.

We are grateful the city leaders of Nagano take such an

interest in us and seek to be helpful in many ways. Even though there is much latent prejudice against Christianity, most people keep it well hidden and others are genuinely interested in Christianity, especially as many were disillusioned after the war with the old religions of Shinto and Buddhism. I often hear older people say, "I am too old to change, but I want my children to go to church and learn about Christianity." I tell them that age doesn't matter for with God "a day is like a thousand years and a thousand years like a day" (Ps 90:4). Perhaps through the children we can also win the parents.

March 17, 1953

Lillian is continuing to study Japanese with a local teacher, Tamura-sensei (who also helps me in my studies). Her schedule is full with Japanese study, helping with the church work, plus all the family and household duties. She could never do this if Shigeko-san wasn't such a competent helper.

Tamura-sensei keeps referring to Shigeko-san as a "maid" but Lillian says I must explain to Tamura-sensei that she is much more than a maid. She often helps me in translating letters and in writing addresses so she helps with secretarial work. Then she is like a governess in the way she cares for and teaches our children. In helping us to plan meals and suggesting ways to do things about the house she is a housekeeper. She is also a seamstress—just yesterday she shortened my pants my mother had sent from America which were too long. We are surprised and pleased at the way she fulfills these multiple roles in our home and she is becoming a dear friend and feels like a member of the family in many ways.

Our bridge across the river washed out again. Last night I had to go out in the pouring rain to get a small can of kerosene as our delivery boy forgot to bring it. With no bridge this meant going a mile out of the way to get to town. Today the delivery lad brought kerosene but he cannot bring the large 50 gallon drum until the bridge is back in. We have heard this might happen by April so people can cross it to the city park during cherry-blossom-viewing time.

Yesterday was the second graduation ceremony of Seikyo Gakuen Junior High School. The celebration lasted five hours, although there were only ten graduates. Everyone enjoyed the lunch together for teachers, students and parents.

Lillian sat through four hours of it which proves she is much stronger than she was a few months ago. She even took six-month old Mary along. Everyone is called upon to do something. I gave them a little pep talk about the promise the future holds for them and Lillian tested their English ability by saying "stand up" in English and then shaking each one's hand and saying: "Congratulations, may God bless you." One part-time teacher did a geisha dance with a fan while we all hummed or sang. Another teacher presented each student with a small drawing which he had made for the occasion.

Easter, 1953

Gradually we are beginning to catch glimpses of what goes on in the inner life of our Japanese community as various ones begin to share with us their problems. One lady came to us Monday and told us about a young man, 18, who took things from her store a couple of times. She wondered if some program in the church could help him. We told her about our church activities and asked her to try to get him to come to the Sunday morning service where he could find Christian friends. The fine young man who washes our car was a teenage victim of the vicious dope traffic that reaches even into small towns like ours. He seems to be recovered now and often comes to church and prayer meeting. Others come to us because they say we look "happy" and they want to know why—which is our opportunity to tell them about Christ.

The new nursery school building we need so badly has begun construction—although it is being built on rented land and partly with borrowed money. Even more exciting is that we now have eleven charter members at the church group in Kaizuka, along with several others attending meetings. Their dream is to have their own land and building someday soon.

March 23, 1953

It may not have been such a good idea to take Mary and Edward to church with us yesterday when I preached at the Tomioka church. Mary cried the whole time and seemed to have a stomach upset. Near the end of the service Edward got the inspiration to bring a large rock into the church and throw it on the floor making enough noise to wake the dead plus scratching the floor that they don't even wear shoes on. Everyone turned to see what had happened and Edward seemed pleased at the attention. Lillian tried to control the situation, but she had to admit that it did wake up the staid and solemn congregation.

Yesterday afternoon two men from Kaizuka came to discuss the possibility of buying a lot for a church there. One they have in mind would cost more than we paid for our house lot but they are sacrificing so admirably we want to encourage them. One man is giving all his savings and they want us to give $600—which would wipe out our savings. We agreed to do our part if the proper lot can be purchased. How can we do less? A bank loan will still be necessary, which we would all help to pay back in monthly installments.

One bright spot in our lives is the occasional box that comes in the mail from folks back home. Recently one came with a toy donkey for Edward (made in Japan), a photo album, mixed dried fruit and some of Lillian's favorite things: mint candy, hand cream and bra pads to use when she nurses Mary. There was baby food for Mary, cookies for Edward (always a favorite) and valentine candy for Shigeko-san. Thrown in for extra measure was a pair of white shoes for Lillian and some material which Lillian is debating whether to make into curtains or dresses for Mary.

March 28, 1953

Lillian shared some of her Christian education knowledge (through an interpreter) with the people in Kaizuka last night and I got up enough courage to pray in Japanese for the second time without a written text. The first time I tried that with some very honest kindergarten kids they laughed at the funny prayer given by the foreigner, which set my public prayer life back quite a bit. Last night no one laughed so I must be improving or else adults are too polite to laugh.

While in Kaizuka yesterday we struck a deal with a former rug maker to buy three of his left over (slightly imperfect) woolen rugs for about one third what a department store would charge. Now that most of the framework for our new missionary home is up we need to start accumulating appropriate furnishings. The rug maker now makes towels and he threw in a few of those as a bonus. One of our Christian friends in Kaizuka introduced us to him and he was so kind to us that Japanese etiquette requires that we take him a return gift when we visit Kaizuka later.

April 6, 1953

We have just returned from a missionary conference in Tokyo where we stayed in a Japanese-style inn. We had only a charcoal *hibachi* for heat, slept on the straw-mat floor, bathed in the Japanese-style tub of hot water and ate Japanese food.

Lillian said she never realized how many times you have to change slippers in a Japanese inn. We wear slippers in the wooden halls but not in the *tatami* (straw mat) rooms. The bath rooms are tile so we have to wear *geta* (wooden clogs) in there and also in the wash rooms which are different from the toilet rooms, which have slippers only to be worn there. All day long it is put on and take off some kind of footwear. Thankfully, the meetings were held in a school and in homes where we were allowed to wear shoes. This was also true for most of the restaurants where we ate.

It was good to see old friends and enjoy the Christian fellowship, study and worship together, but we all returned home with colds. One side benefit of a missionary conference is that we all get a medical checkup by mission doctors—who have to work extra hard to get it all done. Edward enjoyed playing with American children, which was new to him as all his friends in Nagano are Japanese.

We weren't able to get on the morning train home, so had to go in the evening, which meant sitting up all night. We arrived home Saturday morning in time to prepare for a busy Sunday schedule.

April 21, 1953

The Japanese bath seems to be both a blessing and a curse. Shigeko-san says she washed her hair at the public bath and thus caught cold. The eye disease, trachoma, seems to spread primarily though public baths where everyone uses the same water and utensils, bringing only soap, wash cloths and towels from home. The wooden wash basins and stools to sit on while washing off before getting into the common bath water are used by everyone in turn. Of course using the same tub of hot water for dozens of people may be the chief means of infection. Since most Japanese homes are not heated, in the winter the hot bath is the favorite means of getting warmed up and relaxed for going to bed. I enjoy it myself.

Shigeko-san's jaundice and cold seem to be well enough for her to come back to work tomorrow, just in time to keep Lillian from collapsing from the burden of taking care of two babies, housekeeping, language study and church work with only occasional help from a new girl, Amiko-san. She knows so little about Western housekeeping that it takes Lillian longer to teach her than to do the job herself. Shigeko-san is so good that when she is away on sick-leave, as often occurs, we learn to appreciate just how skilled and valuable she is.

April 26, 1953

Our new missionary home is almost half completed but there are details that need counsel. Since it is on a hill, the plumber says we can get enough water pressure to have a shower and a flush toilet if we put a holding tank in the attic which would provide pressure by gravity when the city water pressure is too low. Also since Japanese women like their sinks low, as most of them are short, Lillian is trying to convince the builders to put ours in at 33 inches high. The low sink in this Japanese house makes her back ache from bending over it. The house will be stucco on the outside and the lathing is being nailed on now. The carpenters say they must have the stucco in place before the rainy season begins in June or it won't dry properly.

Since the new house will be only two blocks from the school both Lillian and I can do more for them. Lillian says she can run back and forth and keep up both home and school duties. One of the boons for us in the new home is that it will be big enough for Shigeko-san to live in which means she will be here to help get breakfast and not have to rush off to get a train in the evening before the dishes are done.

Edward, 2, is a great lover of the Japanese *mikan* (mandarin orange). Recently we bought more than usual and piled them high in the refrigerator. He went to get one and was overjoyed at the abundance and came running into the living room with *mikans* in each hand and yelling *"takusan, takusan"* (lots of them). It was a big moment for him to find more *mikans* than he could eat in a week.

May 11, 1953

Edward managed a shy "Happy Mother's Day" to Lillian today. He is certainly not shy in giving his ideas of what is right or wrong. He just gently reminded Lillian that she forgot to put his bib on to eat and he makes sure we don't forget our napkins. We are teaching him the proper names of all the parts of his body and find that he wants to know the Japanese name as well. His Japanese is really better than his English, which is a problem we need to work on.

Our language teacher, Tamura-sensei, recently got married and stopped coming to church. We find many women married to non-Christian men have to give up going to church to please their husbands. However this does not mean they give up their faith. One Japanese lady we know could not go to church for over 50 years but when her husband died she was in church the next Sunday and never misses now unless she is sick. Fortunately, not all men treat their wives this way.

Today we received a $100 gift from one of Lillian's old friends, Miss Emma Hammer. It will help a lot with the increasing church and school expenses but we still wish we could get better housing for our Japanese pastor, Rev. Toru Hashimoto, and his family.

The United Church central office sent new bicycles to rural pastors so he got one and now peddles all over the countryside. He jokingly says that may be why he has high blood pressure, but I think his many church duties cause this so his bicycle exercise should help control it. He and his family certainly make many sacrifices for the work of the church. We help when we can with both church duties and financial needs but it is not enough.

May 24, 1953

Friday will be the first year anniversary of our church work at Kaizuka. The church is growing slowly but steadily, meeting in rather inconvenient rented quarters. We tried to rent a public rental room in a bank but were refused—one of the few times we have faced discrimination toward Christians.

The Izumi-Sano church group convenes in the home of a Christian widow in that conservative textile industry town. We are trying to encourage them to buy land and build their own church and I have agreed to preach for them at least once a month, even though it means a train ride of almost two hours each way with two transfers. In order to do this I will have to give up preaching at Tomioka but they have their own land and building and don't need my help as Izumi-sano and Kaizuka do.

Lillian says I am making more of Kaizuka's anniversary than of our own wedding anniversary which is May 28th. On our anniversary we try to get away at least one night in a quiet Japanese inn with beautiful mountain scenery and hope to make this an annual tradition. Last year it was a thrill to see a wild pheasant walk through the natural garden at the mountain inn we went to on Mt. Rokko, near Kobe. Wild birds are everywhere in Japan but it is rare to see rabbits, squirrels, deer, wild pigs, or badgers, although they do exist. Hokkaido even has bears.

May 31, 1953

Two difficulties of having a car in Japan became apparent this past week. I took a group of pastors to a church meeting in Nara Prefecture on Tuesday morning and on the way to another meeting in Osaka in the afternoon a girl on a bike, carrying a friend on the back of the bike, lost control on the narrow road and fell against my car. The bike owner scraped the skin off her arm when she hit the gravel on the road. She insisted she was all right but we took her to a nearby hospital to have the arm disinfected and bandaged and reported the accident to the police in town.

They turned it over to the county police as it was out of their jurisdiction. It seems the town police control the right side of the road while the county police control the left. It took the county police from four thirty until eleven to take pictures, measure the road and interview all participants and witnesses, after which it was conceded that the accident was caused by the narrow road and slippery gravel and no one was at fault. I didn't get home until the wee hours.

On Thursday in Osaka someone broke the handle off the back door of the car to steal my brief case, leaving several food packages intact. Japanese people usually carry their money in their briefcases. I would like to have seen the face of that thief when he opened my briefcase and found only a Bible and copies of three of my best sermons. I hope it was enough to convert him!

All this put quite a damper on our wedding anniversary but we still managed to get into Osaka and enjoy a steak dinner and the movie, *The Story of Three Loves*. We see a movie so seldom that it was a real treat. I gave Lillian a corsage of three roses and she indulged herself by going to a fancy beauty parlor in Osaka and having her hair and nails done. The local beauty parlors don't do nails.

Today I preached at Yao where I took over from Miss

Verna Hertzler when she retired. Lillian and the children went with me. Their congregation meets in the home of a Christian family, the Yoshizawas, until they can save up enough money to build a church. Mrs. Yoshizawa, whose children are all grown, took over Edward. She fed him cake, bought him tiny wooden *geta*, made him a boat out of a lima bean shell with a match for a mast and also carried him everywhere. He loved it! All this plus getting to play with some Sunday school children made a very happy day for Edward. Mary slept quietly through most of the adventure.

June 14, 1953

There is no escaping death and taxes, even in Japan. I have just learned the "good news" that our income tax was chosen for auditing to make sure we foreigners are paying all we should. Apparently most Japanese find a way to avoid much of the tax. On top of a busy church schedule, car repairs and making plans to move into our new missionary home, this is an unwelcome waste of time but I have to take my lumps along with the Japanese.

Actually we have little to complain about as the Japanese have treated us more kindly than we expected, considering their natural bitterness at being defeated in the war. We are certainly treated much better here than many foreigners are back home. It makes us a little ashamed at the comparison.

The Nagano church has just bought a "fixer upper" home for Pastor Hashimoto's family and we have committed ourselves to pay ¥15,000 ($42) down and ¥5,000 ($14) a month until the repairs are completed. It's going to be a struggle making ends meet but it isn't forever and we can cut down on a few luxuries for a time. The Hashimotos have sacrificed a lot more for the ministry here than we have—as have many of the church members.

June 29, 1953

Edward fell into a sewage ditch this morning while we were waiting for the car to be repaired in Tondabayashi.

Falling backward he didn't get his face in the water but he looked horrible and his clothing smelled of human excrement. The garage man loaned us a man's undershirt to put on him while we gave him a good washing and soaked his clothing. In Osaka we bought him a new outfit. After a nap and the new outfit, the world looked a lot brighter to him, and to us.

Asking Japanese carpenters to build a Western-style house has its hazards. After the struggle to get higher sinks installed, I found they had used opaque glass on my bookcase so none of the books could be seen. Then the hanging light over the dining room table and the ceiling light in the breakfast nook were reversed. Getting some color into the drab outside stucco walls was a struggle and the wooden panels I wanted on the bottom of doors turned out to be opaque glass from top to bottom. However, on the whole we are very pleased with our new missionary home and hope to move in on July 13th.

Yesterday the family went with me to preach and for a picnic on the beach in Izumi-Sano. After this we went on to the first Sunday school meeting of the Kaizuka group. So few children showed up for Sunday school that a church member and I went through the neighborhood distributing leaflets and soon 50 children appeared. It is usually easy to get a crowd of children together in Japan.

The pastor in these churches is a fine man but he seems to think he can merely supervise without actively engaging in the work himself and still get things done. I have to do a lot of pushing and encouraging with him, not like with Pastor Hashimoto who is a real go-getter.

On the way home yesterday Lillian drove the car until we met a bus. The road was too narrow, so she started backing up to let it pass and somehow we almost backed over a cliff into a river. Fortunately only one back wheel went over and with help from men in the bus we were able to get the car back on the road. Lillian said she would never drive again.

Something was damaged in the process so we had to push the car to get it over every hill until we got home, late at night. We were all exhausted.

July 5, 1953

This has been an exciting week. First was the laying of the cornerstone for the new church building in Tondabayashi. They won't have to meet in homes or rented quarters much longer. Then our architect-evangelist, Merril Vories Hitotsuyanagi came for dinner. He autographed the hymn he wrote, "Let There Be Light, Lord God of Hosts" in our hymnal and gave his final blessing on our new missionary home which he designed in preparation for our moving in next Friday.

After dinner I took him to Kaizuka for a special evangelistic meeting where he told how he had been inspired to come to Japan as a missionary by John R. Mott. He had heard Dr. Mott say, "The world has yet to see what a young man can do who dares to follow Christ, come what may." Vories said to himself, "I am going to try that." As a result he left architectural school and came to Japan as a YMCA worker.

Over the succeeding years he won hundreds to Christ through his work in the conservative Buddhist and Shinto area of Omi Hachiman in Kyoto Prefecture. There he married a Japanese lady of the nobility class, taking her family name, Hitotsuyanagi (One Willow) and became a Japanese citizen and thus was the only missionary allowed to stay free in Japan during the war. His mentholatum factory was seen as essential to the war efforts, so not only was his factory allowed to stay open, but the military even permitted his Christian work to go on with some restrictions.

His stories deeply impressed the people at Kaizuka and won new prospects for the church. After the meeting I took him to a hotel in Osaka and finally got home about two in the morning. He told me privately that just before visiting us he had a phone call from the younger prince in the royal family saying he had just won his sister and a school friend to Christianity, but they are keeping it secret because of their delicate position in Japanese affairs.

Driskill family in Western
dress

Shigedo Okuda with
one-year-old Edward

Edward and Mary
in festival dress

Driskill family in Japanese dress

清教の明日を語る

1984 5 12

Seikyo Gakuen meeting with Driskills

Senri Newtown, a "bed-town" for Osaka of 150,0000 people

View of Seikyo Gakuen Christian School in 1984

Seikyo Gakuen's first
board of directors

Teachers of Seikyo Gakuen
Christian School

Students from special English language classes

Driskills being honored by members of Seikyo Gakuen school

Lillian and Grandmother
Morikawa baptized at 80

Christian Pavilon at
1970 World's Fair in Osaka

The Tondabayashi church

The Osaka Jogakuin High School and Junior College

Dedication celebration of
Seikyo Gakuen High School's new campus

Early picture of
Senri Newton church

Women of Senri Newton church
in 1984 with the Driskills

The Misasagi church

The Tomioka church

The Hatsushiba church

The Kaizuka church

The Senri Newtown church in 1984

The Semboku Newtown church

Japanese young people
at the Kawachinagano church

Driskill speaking at the Kawachinagano
church in 1984

A typical home meeting in Senri Newtown

Ayame Nursery School

Driskills visiting with leaders of Osaka Jogakuin in 1984

Buffet dinner given in honor of Driskill, May, 1984

III

Putting Down Roots

July 12, 1953

We moved into our new home Friday. Lillian said she almost cried the first time she used her beautiful new kitchen with a fluorescent light right over the sink. In the old kitchen she had been bumping her head on a naked light bulb hung too low over the sink. Although the bridge across the river is out again, the students from Seikyo Gakuen helped us carry things across. For the heavy furniture—couch, beds and appliances we hired a big truck with three men to carry things. They carried the refrigerator across the river by hand to the truck on the other side. Thanks to them and the wonderful help from church and school people, moving was not as bad as we had anticipated. For their refreshment I went out and bought ice cream, cold drinks and cookies.

Last Monday we had a beautiful day at Hamadera Beach with the Hashimotos. Even the car axle breaking for the second time couldn't spoil our good outing even though Edward has been paying the price ever since with a flaming red sunburn.

On Thursday Mrs. Hashimoto went into the hospital and had several polyps removed from her womb, but she certainly didn't let their presence bother her at the beach outing, nor did the bumpy ride home in a *shita-kiri* (tongue-cutting) bus seem to do her any harm. When told that the polyps were like grapes, Pastor Hashimoto said, "How interesting, I am the father of a bunch of grapes."

Shigeko-san was not able to move in with us because just then her mother complained of being "sick." Shigeko-san thinks it is mostly psychological since her mother hates to see her leave home, even though she is in her twenties and it is only 15 minutes away by train. We are beginning to understand why the mother annulled her marriage after a few days.

Our cat also showed psychological damage from the move. We brought him over in a box (not more than a mile from his old home) but he refused to go outside the house until we took him out by force. He didn't run back to the old home though and seemed greatly relieved when we let him back inside. Edward is the opposite—we have to force him to come in from playing outside in our roomy new yard.

We have been taking cold showers but today they fixed the Japanese hot water heater so tomorrow we should have hot water for showers and the laundry. After playing outside with new neighbor children Edward is always badly in need of a bath before bed time. He is probably our best "missionary" as he can get into homes we cannot enter. The neighbors love children and he opens a lot of doors for us, as does Mary as she "strolls" around the neighborhood.

One of our neighbors has T.B. as does our missionary friend, Jane Simpson. With reasonable care we think we can protect the children. We have to take X-rays annually and I show I have been exposed to it by antibodies and lung scars, but I do not have it now. The Japanese are careful to wear surgical masks when they go outside even with a cold, so they take extra care with T.B. During the war many here got it, so everyone has to be careful. Improved nutrition and health care seem to help win the battle.

July 19, 1953, Sunday

Lillian says she still can't believe we are actually living in our new house. Today we all went out for the first time and she said "I keep feeling like we should stop in to check on the new house on the way home," which is what we have been doing for several months. We feel like plutocrats, especially being able to drive our car right up to the house and park in our own garage instead of across the river and using a footbridge (or else walking a mile out of our way to the car bridge on a path leading from there to our old home).

Since we moved into our new house just after the rainy season we do not have to do the usual housecleaning most do here to remove mildew. The custom is to choose one day for the whole neighborhood to clean house at the same time. It makes sense since everyone lives so closely together that one person's cleaning might interfere with another's work.

On cleaning day the families take out their *tatami* (straw mats) and beat the dust out of them and then sun them. *Tatami* is much heavier than rugs so the men have to help clean them and all day long you can hear the sound of the beating of the *tatami* around you. It happens twice a year—and the time after the rainy season is especially crucial since everything tends to mildew and must be cleaned before it rots.

Lillian says she can't get used to spring cleaning in July or to flooding bathroom floors rather than scrubbing them Western style. The custom here is to throw cold water on the bathroom floor and swish it down the drain. Two ladies who helped clean our new house when we moved in were really upset when water wouldn't gush out the small drain in the bathroom floor. They were up to their ankles in water before they realized that we scrub instead of flood.

My annual evangelistic caravan with seminary students and local pastors begins tomorrow when we visit towns and villages to hold mass meetings where there is no church or where the church needs special help. We usually have gatherings for children in the morning and afternoon using *bunraku* puppets to tell Biblical stories. Then we have services for adults at night. We carry a portable organ for singing and give an evangelistic message, usually by our best speaker who has had extensive evangelistic experience. Last year we toured places in Nara Prefecture and this year we are going to the Osaka Prefecture which means the traveling team will be able to return in the evening and spend the night in our new home.

Aug. 4, 1953—Lake Nojiri

Vacationing here at Lake Nojiri has provided us a welcome respite from the busy week of our evangelistic caravan where we had as many as three meetings a day. The Nojiri Lake Association is a fellowship of missionaries from many countries joined together to form this summer vacation retreat and owns all the land. We each must build or buy our own summer cabin. At present there are 120 cabins here housing some 500 people from America and Europe.

The lake is small but adequate—over a mile wide and two miles long with lovely bays and inlets leading back into small mountain valleys. The water comes from snowmelt and underground springs but it warms up enough so you can swim in July and August. The lake's elevation is 2,500 feet and the average temperature for August, the hottest month, is 77°. There are four clay tennis courts plus a primitive 9-hole golf course. Hiking around the lake takes two to three hours, depending on how fast one walks. Our cabin is a steep climb up from the lake which is a hard pull for Edward. Yesterday after we climbed up I asked him if he was tired and he said "Yes, I much walked!"

The cabins have no running water; bathrooms are sheds built onto the side of each one with a holding tank which the farmers empty every couple days to use for fertilizer on their farms. Instead of a refrigerator we use snow caves. Winter snows sometimes pile up to two or three feet and we pay local men to shovel it off the roofs so they won't cave in from the weight and this provides plenty of snow for the cave.

Nearby Mt. Kurohime (Black Princess) and Mt. Myoko provide mountain climbing opportunities and there are many lower hiking trails here in Nagano Prefecture. Small and medium earthquakes occur several times a year but usually do little damage. A few cabins are winterized so some come up for winter skiing, but they usually have to walk in from a train or bus line over a mile away since snow blocks the road in. Fellowship, Bible study groups, worship services and occasionally Christian conferences are available to all.

Aug. 17, 1953

Tomorrow there are boat and swimming races planned plus a community picnic in the evening down by the water. I have learned indirectly that Lillian is giving a party for my 33rd birthday at our cabin with the Presbyterian "Ds" (the Daubs, Drummonds, Davises and Driskills). I was in real need of this vacation as I have just learned from the missionary doctor here that my hemoglobin is low and I need vitamins. Unfortunately I have succumbed to the plague of boils that have hit some here. With all the streptococcus bacteria around it doesn't take much drop in resistance to get these painful boils. I can still play golf and tennis but can't go into the water above my waist as the boils are on my shoulder.

At the annual meeting the other day someone wanted to divide his lot and build a second cabin on it. Since one of the attractions here is getting away from the crowds and enjoying a bit of nature, many fear this could become another Coney Island if we divide lots indiscriminately. In any case, it engendered some lively discussion. It looks as if a minimum size for lots will be worked out to prevent overcrowding.

The Youth for Christ conference was held in Tokyo last week and was quite effective, we hear. Some from here went down for it, but we decided to limit our worship, study and fellowship to the opportunities provided right here.

Sept. 13, 1953—Nagano

At the annual retreat of our Nagano church held in a quiet country inn we learned some of the special problems Japanese Christians face. One woman pointed out that when all the family are not Christian it is often impossible to remove the images of Buddhism and Shinto from the home, out of respect for the non-Christian members of the family. Every home is supposed to have a *Kamidana* (Shinto god-shelf) and *Butsuden* (Buddhist shrine) and most homes do.

One devout Christian woman said she faces similar criticism from surrounding relatives who would accuse her of breaking family tradition if she removes the images, as she would like to do. Another believer said she felt obligated to go along with Buddhist memorial services for the dead held by non-Christian relatives since they reproved her for being unsympathetic and disrespectful when she did not take part.

Even more subtle are the neighborhood festivals and community fees which have Shinto or Buddhist roots, but which most people claim are now just "community affairs" but which all are obligated to support. In our community the fee is used for helping any whose house burns down or is damaged by a typhoon and for those with extra expenses due to an illness or for other reasons of poverty. We have been contributing since we understood it to be a neighborhood charity fund which all should support and were a bit chagrined to learn later that the fund is also used for an annual gift to support the local Buddhist temple. How does one handle these problems, especially if you are under pressure from non-Christian relatives and friends?

One of our Nagano elders was adopted into a Shinto family but was the only one who became a Christian. When the father died the family demanded a Shinto funeral. Out of respect for him and to support this elder, several of us also attended the funeral. The corpse was buried in a sitting/fetal position in a wooden barrel-shaped casket. Before being interred in the ground the casket was put on a revolving pedestal and whirled around.

When I later asked Pastor Hashimoto what that meant he explained it was to confuse the spirit of the dead man so he will not come back to haunt the family or friends, especially anyone whom he disliked or felt had wronged him. Most people are cremated after death in Japan but an occasional burial of the body does still take place.

How to maintain one's Christian convictions and still show proper respect for the living and the dead is a dilemma here. One compromise in the case of Christian relatives who die is to have a Christian memorial service for them observing the one month and one year anniversary schedule of Buddhism, but using only Christian content for the service.

The first time I attended a Christian funeral and saw Christians talking to a large picture of the deceased placed beside the casket I was a bit concerned. However, when I asked about it, a Japanese Christian answered, "We believe he is still alive and immortal. Don't you?" I felt properly rebuked for an insensitive question.

Sept. 29, 1953

Our worst typhoon since coming to Japan occurred Friday. I was away for a week's conference in Tokyo so Lillian, Shigeko-san and the kids had to brave it alone. Lillian says the principal of Seikyo Gakuen school warned her when she went to teach that morning that the worst part was expected after lunch. Two other people from the church also came to warn her for they were worried our big windows might break.

They didn't break but the wind was blowing the rain horizontally so hard that all of the windows leaked around the edges and even the air vent in the attic let in enough water to run through the ceiling of Mary's bedroom. Shigeko-san climbed into the attic to stuff towels into the vent. In the excitement her feet slipped off the joist and came through the ceiling of Mary's room. Lillian said it was a strange sensation to see a foot suddenly come through the ceiling, pushing fragments of plaster board ahead of it. Fortunately Shigeko-san's pride was the only thing hurt and we had a good laugh together about it later. Of course the foot bridge to our old house washed out again and the river flooded into the basement rooms. We were glad we had moved to higher ground.

On my way home by train from Tokyo I saw much of the big city of Nagoya under water. Huge timbers, dead cows, pigs and pets floated on the muddy water. I was deeply distressed by the sight of so many flooded homes and homeless people. Hurricanes and earthquakes make Japan an exciting, but sometimes dangerous, place to live. Lillian said in the worst part of the typhoon at about three in the afternoon a fearful tremor shook the entire house. Needless to say everyone's nerves where badly shaken by the time I got home.

I even got some of my train fare back because my train was almost four hours late, delayed by flood water.

Our city water system was out for several days. Fortunately we could get drinking water from a neighbor's well.

Oct. 4, 1953

Yesterday we finally got over to see how our former landlord's family fared in the typhoon. Their place is almost in ruins. A week after the flood Mr. Hayakawa was still trying to clean out the mud and repair the damage to the house. Three houses on the riverbank were completely washed away. All they get to help from flood relief funds is ¥2,000 ($6) plus some voluntary help with repairs if the house is repairable. The Hayakawas are living temporarily in the part of the house we formerly occupied for it will be a long time before they can clean out the mud and repair their adjoining quarters.

Lillian's asthma is much worse, perhaps from all the stress of the past week. Both of us are badly in need of rest and sleep. Since many of my meetings are at distant places I often don't get home until after midnight and now when colds and coughing awaken the children, we have to get up with them at night, which makes it rough on both of us.

When I told Lillian I had seen her hometown pastor, Dr. Charles Leber, in Tokyo, she admitted that for the first time, the strain of the past week had made her feel homesick and not being able to see him made it worse. Maybe she will get a chance to see him on his way back from Hong Kong as he passes through Osaka.

One good bit of news among all the trials and tribulations is that this afternoon Tondabayashi dedicated their new church building. All of us stretched our budgets to the limit to make it possible, so we are not eating quite as well as we formerly did. Maybe that's one reason we feel tired and get colds so easily. I am sure things will improve soon.

Oct. 12, 1953

Saturday night Lillian had another asthma attack that kept

her up for about three hours. Fortunately Dr. Sawada is nearby and I can call him in an emergency for an asthma shot, which I recently had to do at five in the morning. His willingness to make house calls is a boon since Lillian cannot make it to his small hospital when she is having a bad attack.

Lillian feels we are beginning to settle and put down roots here, yet there is still an element of homesickness about our life. The honeymoon stage of the glamour and fascination of living in exotic Japan is over and we now have to get on with the nitty-gritty job of Christian life and service in Japan. God never promised missionary life would be easy, but we have been blessed in seeing so many new churches developed and many won to Christ.

We must trust God to give us the endurance necessary to continue to meet the opportunities and challenges that lie ahead. At times it is harder on the missionary wife who has to make a home under difficult conditions without participating as directly in seeing the immediate results of Christian work that the husband observes almost daily in his church work. Also having to do all her writing by hand since our typewriter was stolen has not helped reduce Lillian's burdens.

Oct. 20, 1953

Edward's third birthday celebration was a big success. When he saw all his gifts he was speechless—an almost unheard of experience for him. Four Garrisons, four Hashimotos and we all came bearing gifts. When everyone sang "Happy Birthday" Edward was too embarrassed for a moment to blow out the candles on his cake. He blushed red but recovered well enough to eat heartily the chicken pie, green beans, lettuce and tomato salad, bread, ice cream, cake and peanuts. His gifts were a small ball and glove, tennis racquet, chalkboard, toy car, a Biblical picture, *geta* and *tabi*, plus a record. This morning he is "cooking" a cake for a party of his own.

Oct. 25, 1953

Hearing the news that Dr. Leber would be coming to see

us tonight, Lillian went this morning to Osaka to get her hair and nails done. I met her after lunch so we could do our Christmas shopping as things must be mailed now to reach America in time. We grabbed a hamburger and a fruit sundae, saw the movie "Hans Christian Anderson" and just had time to meet Dr. Leber and Paul Oltman at eight.

Dr. Leber was well received by our Tondabayashi and Nagano churches where he spoke. He said he will have been away from home for five months when he returns in November! From here he goes to Korea. Lillian was so pleased with the visit, she cried when he left. By then she had forgiven his refusing her apple pie going-to-bed snack and felt having him visit was almost like having her parents come since he is the family pastor. Frankly, he was a little crotchety for my taste.

Nov. 1, 1953

Being a Baltimore Oriole fan Lillian loves baseball. To cheer her up I offered to take her to see the All American Team play the Nankai Hawks in Osaka Friday. Lillian was "thrilled" for she had been wanting to see a game for two years. We lunched at the stadium in Osaka to be sure of getting seats, but then had to wait almost two hours for the opening festivities. Fortunately we were armed with newspapers and magazines so the time passed quickly.

In the opening exercises planes buzzed the stadium and we felt, since we were high in the stands, they were right over our heads. The army band provided stirring music yet it was strange to hear our national anthem being played. Many Japanese joined us and the other Americans who stood up and we all stood again for the Japanese anthem. Some lovely Japanese girls presented flowers to the American team who stood on the third base line while the Hawks stood on the first base line. The Hawks stood erectly in a straight line but the Americans were all over the place looking around and taking pictures, individualism personified. The preliminaries were more interesting than the game which was a 15-1 rout by the Americans. It brought back good home memories for

Lillian, who thought it was well worth it.

We got home just in time to enjoy a Halloween supper with the children. Shigeko-san hollowed out a pumpkin and cut a face as Lillian had taught her to do. This was the centerpiece around which we ate our candlelight supper rounded off with pumpkin pie. Lillian brought out some old masks for everyone to put on and it was a lot of fun, especially for the younger set.

Last month when Lillian and I went visiting the sick with Pastor Hashimoto we were a little surprised to find that of the four homes we visited three had someone ill with T.B. We now understand why mission doctors insist we have a chest X-ray every year. It is all around us. I visit a T.B. sanitarium for worship services regularly and we always gargle and wash our hands carefully when we get home.

My mother and father have offered to send us money to buy a typewriter and we are overjoyed as we need one badly.

Nov. 10, 1953

It is getting chilly here and I got out all the heaters in preparation. We are using the electric heater in the bathroom and kerosene stoves in the other rooms. The large two-burner with a smoke pipe is in the living room, an old portable is in the kitchen with a newer one in my study plus one we bought from Mrs. Hannaford in Shigeko-san's room. She will probably use it very rarely as most Japanese people are accustomed to having no heat at all in their bedroom.

Sunday morning we went to church and found Dr. Sawada there inoculating all the small children against diphtheria. One child has died of it and two others are now ill. Dr. Sawada says this kind also weakens the heart. We had Edward inoculated again but Mary just received hers in April so we think she will be all right. Lillian's mother sent a new snowsuit for Edward. His old one fits Mary, a bit generously, but we are about ready for winter. Mary's outgrown snowsuit has gone to our language teacher Yagi-sensei's new baby.

Nov. 17, 1953

Lillian had her missionary baptism by fire Sunday. For the first time she taught a Sunday school class of pre-schoolers without help because the assistant never showed up. It went well for the first hour and just when she thought classes were over, a new bunch of older youngsters come in expecting to be taught. In the confusion of trying to integrate them with the nursery age children, one nursery school boy ran off without his wooden *geta*. She couldn't leave the others to go after him and so worried whether he would get home all right. After the second class she asked Tsujino-sensei to go with her to check on him and was greatly relieved to find him safely at home.

Then after that she was asked to join the ladies of the church in carrying bricks from the factory to the new nursery school to build a large sandbox for the children. They were carrying them in baby carriages and small two-wheeled carts. This went on for two hours followed by refreshments of tea, candy, cookies and sweet potatoes provided by the daughter of the president of the factory. He had donated the bricks free since they had imperfections in them. Unfortunately Lillian strained herself in the process and lost all her supper.

Nov. 22, 1953

Lillian felt successful today. She taught 14 nursery-age children in Sunday school and survived the hectic time so well she said, "What a wonderful opportunity to teach the love of Christ!" She has also become an accomplished hostess for our weekly Tuesday night open house sessions, serving cocoa, cookies and peanuts while I try to answer the young people's questions about the Bible, Christianity, or life in America. Anyone is welcome but it is usually high school and college age students who come. For some this is their first contact with Christianity and a few move on from the open house to attending church and becoming believers. One young man has made his decision to become a Christian pastor.

Lillian and I will also host five missionary friends for a

Thanksgiving dinner on Thursday. Friday and Saturday we go to Kobe for a two-day missionary conference.

At least one out of every ten members in our Nagano church has T.B. Recently one member died of it leaving a wife and three small children. Seeing his courage, we were impressed with the peace and joy Christ can give even to those who know they are soon to die. His dying words were, "Pastor, we know when death is near, don't we . . . everything seems completely different . . . I was blessed!"

The sacrificial spirit of Japanese Christians is truly impressive. One young woman from the Tondabayashi church works as a maid for her room and board and $15 a month and gives three dollars of this to help pay for the new church building. Two young girls from the new group at Kaizuka travel over an hour by train to join our teacher training classes. A widow who works as a cook in a nursery school, and sometimes as a maid, uses her day off to teach church school classes in surrounding villages where there is no church.

Dec. 6, 1953

All Sundays are busy, but today was even more so. As soon as Lillian had taught her morning class at Nagano church we left by car to get to Yao in time for me to preach at 10:30. After a wonderful *sukiyaki* dinner in the home where the church meets, we went on to Osaka for a glorious presentation of Handel's *Messiah* at the Jo Gakuin (girls' school) followed by a brief supper of waffles and coffee at Alice Grube's home. After eating a quarter of a waffle I had to leave for a congregational meeting at Tondabayashi and enroute had to switch from car to train when the headlights failed.

Dec. 13, 1953

We had 25 Sunday school teachers at our home for special training today. Although one expected guest speaker never showed up we had two seminary-trained Christian educators speak—one of them being Lillian who majored in Christian education at Princeton Theological Seminary for three years.

Crullers, coffee, Japanese cookies and *mikans* were provided for the teachers to munch on as they absorbed new ideas about how to teach children about God' creation, God's love and God's will for our lives and work better.

We had to borrow twelve coffee cups from our neighbors as we had only 13. Although Lillian and I were exhausted from too much Christmas partying with fellow missionaries in Osaka last night (getting home past midnight) we still managed to make this a good learning experience for them.

Edward was so tired from getting in late plus having a cold, that he slept through most of the day. I empathized with him for I was so fatigued this morning I felt my preaching lacked the usual enthusiasm I try to put into it.

Dec. 20, 1953

As usual the Christmas season is a golden opportunity for witnessing here and we are trying to make the most of it. Today I was away for Christmas meetings the entire day and the same will be true tomorrow. Last year we had over 20 Christmas celebrations in churches, homes, schools and factories and it looks like there may be more this year. They usually continue right up to New Year's Day when for three or four days the traditional Japanese New Year's event is celebrated.

For them this means paying all debts by the first, throwing beans around the house to chase off evil spirits, cleaning house, cooking up endless goodies for a series of family celebrations and visiting family and friends. Perhaps the most important custom of all is for all employees to go to their boss with a gift and say, *"Akemashite, omedetoo gozaimasu. Dozo, kotoshi mo yoroshiku"* (Congratulations and best wishes for the New Year. Please continue to grant me your favor). Students do the same for their teachers, and some students and church members do the same for us.

The greatest Christmas treat for Lillian has been the purchase of a 93-piece set of dishes, which we badly need, plus a used Royal typewriter which we bought with my parents' gift. It needs cleaning badly but is otherwise O.K.

Last night we stopped at a marine base near here and invited two fellows to come for Christmas dinner. We have been wanting to do it for a long time but never got around to it.

Dec. 27, 1953

Our home celebration began Christmas Eve with 150 guests—students and adults—crowding into our new house for a brief service. Our dining room and living room were so full everyone had to stand for the service as there was not room to sit down! For refreshments we relayed them through the kitchen, out into the hall and into the living room. Some left then so the rest sat down on the floor and we had some stunts and fun songs.

Everyone had gone caroling before they came here but we were busy getting ready so didn't go. We served cocoa. Lillian bought 50 cheap Japanese tea cups which we used and kept washing. The girls of the church all helped. Lillian had a bad time serving as she had an infection under her left thumbnail, which later kept her awake all night.

At seven Christmas morning she went to the doctor but he was still asleep and his wife didn't think it was important enough to wake him up. At ten she returned and his assistant removed the thumbnail to get at the infection underneath. Needless to say she is handicapped now and I am preparing to do most of the work next week as we can't get any help over New Year's—a mandatory holiday season for everyone.

On my way home from church today I stopped at the marine base and found that three marines wanted to have dinner with us today. Lillian had expected two but she managed the surprise. The Hashimoto family arrived soon after we did. After dinner the two unmarried fellows went for a walk with me to deliver our present to our former landlords, the Hayakawas.

Shigeko-san and Mrs. Hashimoto did the dishes while Lillian attended a Sunday school party and the married marine (who has two children) acted as the babysitter. He went out to the garage and got wood to build a fire in the fireplace and then played the guitar for the ten children present who loved every minute of it.

In the afternoon Lillian and I went to Kaizuka for a Christmas party leaving Shigeko-san and Mrs. Hashimoto entertaining the marines until seven in the evening. They played ping-pong and Chinese checkers, sang carols and drank lots of coffee. I think the ladies enjoyed it as much as the marines. They left us a thank-you note saying we are a "wonderful" family. They were all Catholics—Irish, Italian and French—but we Protestants got along well with them. The ladies couldn't speak English and the marines couldn't speak Japanese, but apparently they had a great time talking (communicating) for three hours after we left. We wished we could have listened in.

This has been an encouraging year. Izumi-Sano has bought land for a church but can't build until we raise $1,500. The Tondabayashi group has already dedicated their first church building. The Izumi-Otsu group still meets in a home but has plans to buy land and build a church. Tondabayashi and Yao hope to call much-needed pastors soon but now have only about half enough income to pay their salaries. Seikyo Gakuen Christian School is growing and desperately needs more land and buildings. All of us are moving ahead on faith, believing that what we need the Lord will provide, in God's own time.

Jan. 3, 1954

On the first we entered the year of the "horse" and left behind the year of the "serpent" according to Japan's zodiac calendar. Japan welcomed the New Year in various ways: 16 were killed mobbing the palace grounds trying to see the emperor; on the train to Kaizuka I had the loving attention of drunks on all sides and today drunks still crowd the trains and many cars on the roads are filled with them. It is a good time to stay home but I felt I should support the non-drinking Christian group in Kaizuka for worship and celebration on New Year's night.

Thursday I attended the New Year's Eve service at Nagano church and spoke at the morning service on New Year's Day. Being nearby I didn't have to face the carousing crowd on trains to get there, but just had to walk five blocks past homes where families and friends were endlessly toasting each other with hot rice wine.

After the New Year's Eve service Lillian and I sat up playing games we had gotten for Christmas and eating pumpkin pie. Edward's cold and earache got too much for him and just at midnight he awoke and vomited all over his bed. We welcomed the New Year in cleaning up the mess. Lillian's infected left thumb still bothers her so I have been doing all the dish washing and potato peeling for the past week. I will be glad to welcome our helper back from vacation on Tuesday.

We received an interesting gift today from the Yao church, a *sukiyaki* set which consists of four rice bowls, a pan to cook the meat and vegetables in, two large platters to hold the raw vegetables and meat before cooking plus containers for soy sauce *(shoyu)*, sugar and water, along with a wooden spatula for serving the rice into the bowls. Lillian thinks it is a treasure and I am sure Shigeko-san will like it also.

Jan. 10, 1954

After Sunday school and worship where I preached, teachers from most of our nine local Sunday schools met in the afternoon at our home for another teacher training event. We asked each one of them to evaluate their own teaching program and in the process learned a great deal from them as they shared the problems, challenges and triumphs of each class they taught. It is almost impossible to keep up with all the Sunday schools but sharing experiences and thoughts like this helps us all. In addition Lillian has been asked to give Christian education training to the kindergarten teachers.

Edward and Mary do a lot of sharing of their toys with about ten children who play here all the time, making good use of our spacious yard. In some ways they do better missionary work than Lillian and I do.

Our medical doctor is now in bed recuperating from an appendix operation. When I visit him he seems open to discussing Christianity, being free of the usual pressures of his work. He says that his scientific training makes it hard for him to believe in God and the Bible but he is impressed by the way a converted school friend of his faced his own death last month. The day before he died he calmly said, "Everyone's busy getting ready for my funeral, aren't they," demonstrating a Christian composure that Dr. Sawada admired. One of his nephews is a Christian, his brother-in-law is an elder and his daughter often attends church. It may take a long time but we are praying that he soon will accept Christ as his personal Lord and Savior. As an outstanding community leader, he could be a real key in leading many others to Christ.

Jan. 17, 1954

A busy week. Wednesday and Thursday we practiced English skits which we presented Friday at the school's PTA program—which lasted from ten until four! Friday night we had a Japanese minister here for dinner and the night. Saturday was the big wedding we have all been waiting for—Shigeko-san's best friend, Takeda-san, and Fujita-sensei, a teacher at our school. Because of health problems they have been waiting three years to get married. It was done in Western-style with a few Japanese customs thrown in. It was a love marriage but they still used the traditional "go-between" to arrange affairs between the two families and escort the bride and groom down the aisle. After the ceremony the couple met in a private room with the immediate family where their health and happiness were toasted with wine. Then they met with all of us for a box containing a small decorated cake with the word "Marriage" on top. Tea and cookies were also served.

Tsuji-san, a high-school boy, stayed with our children so we could go. Mary slept the whole time and Edward played outside. Mary woke up just as we came home but she wasn't crying as she knows Tsuji-san and likes him very much. Today I was up at the crack of dawn and off to the coast towns, Izumi-Sano and Kaizuka, for worship services. I managed not to fall asleep at the wheel but my plans to sleep in tomorrow were thrwarted when a telegram arrived today saying I am needed at a meeting in Osaka.

Jan. 24, 1954

Our small one room, one teacher, nursery school is in danger. A secular social service agency wants to build a larger one in connection with an "old folks home." Two cannot be in the same area, and although ours is older the bigger money-backing and promises of the secular group may force us to move elsewhere. It is particularly irritating that the leader of the secular group is a former Episcopal priest who gave up church work when things got rough for churches during the war and moved on to the easier, government-backed, social work field.

Our contact with the little children opens the door for us into almost every home in Nagano so we could lose one of our vital contacts with the people. Whatever the outcome, we trust God will help us continue the nursery school work in some appropriate way. In today's congregational meeting, the members reminded me of the early Christians, showing much faith and determination. With such a strong Christian spirit no wonder they have accomplished so much with their limited financial resources.

A Norwegian Christian education specialist spoke to 21 of our teachers this afternoon as part of the continuing teacher-training program held in our home. She was quite fluent in Japanese and did a good job. It was so late when we finished Lillian invited her and Yamashita-san, who brought her, to stay for supper. Lillian enjoyed the "English conversation," which is a welcome break from constant Japanese speaking, plus this insight into Christian education in Norway.

Shigeko-san broke the news this week that she wants to leave the end of February. Her mother needs her to do laundry, she says, but we think another major reason is that she wants to get married again. She seems to be recovered from the unhappy one that was annulled by her strong-minded mother, with the father going along to keep peace in the family. Since Shigeko-san is adopted she is tightly controlled by her mother, a very excitable, nervous type. One problem is that the new husband must also be adopted to carry on the family name so he is scrutinized even more carefully than is usual.

Feb. 1, 1954

Last Saturday Lillian and I went to the dentist in Osaka and found we will have to go at least three or four more times to get our neglected teeth in shape again. That is the price we pay for waiting three years—since leaving America—before having our teeth checked.

We have about half enough money to buy land for a church in Kaizuka but both land and rent prices are very high. Even to rent we have to make a down payment (deposit) which amounts to about half the purchase price—which appears to be standard practice here in Japan.

It is very cold and windy. Light snow fell a few days ago and last night hail almost as large as marbles fell.

Feb. 7, 1954

Airmail to the U.S. is moving quite well now. It usually takes five or six days but my mother just wrote that our last letter reached her in three days. Our new second-hand typewriter is so valuable to us that I lock it up in my office closet every night. Break-ins were so common in our old neighborhood we learned to be very careful, but none have occurred in our new house. I wonder if it has anything to do with being near a Buddhist temple which might scare off superstitious thieves.

Recently our friends, the Duntons, had an armed robber break into their home near Tokyo demanding money and valuables. They jumped on the robber, the pistol went off and shot a hole in the floor before they finally subdued him and sat on him until the police came. They are both nervous types and the traumatic experience upset them so much that we now hear they must return to the States, perhaps permanently.

I have been doing some counseling with a one-legged thief who has been in jail twelve times for stealing. I know he sometimes carries a pistol but he has never threatened me or stolen anything here, even though I have given him part-time work and let him sleep on our couch occasionally. He is an alcoholic with a violent temper who has threatened our Japanese pastor.

One day he and another petty criminal were demanding money from our pastor and two elders at the church. They called me to come and talk to him. When I arrived he went into a long harangue about how Japan has no racial prejudice unlike America which he considered the most racist nation in the world. Apparently he ignores the treatment of Koreans and outcast people here. Another day he telephoned asking me to meet him at the railroad station as the police had forbidden him to come to my home. It was late at night and dark around the station, so it was a bit scary to go there but, hoping he would someday be converted, I went. He asked for train fare back to his home village where he can get welfare help, so I gave it to him.

As in America, churches here are favorite targets for the needy. Some are genuine hardship cases but most are panhandlers. Fearing I might fail to aid someone with genuine needs, I usually try to help.

Yesterday we found Edward had expelled an intestinal worm, a common problem in Japan. At age three he can't understand why he has to take medication and go without food until noon today. When Lillian gave other kids cookies at Sunday school today he said "Give me one to put in my pocket." If he can't put it in his stomach his pocket is the next best spot. He was greatly impressed when a new student put ¥20 into the offering when most kids put in only ten.

Japanese custom prohibits mixed parties for young single

people. Therefore, we were pleasantly surprised when the newlywed Takeda-san, who is now Mrs. Fujita, announced that she was having a mixed singles party for her close friends. Having managed a love marriage with her husband she seems led to become a matchmaker for others. I wonder if her Christian faith is what gives her the courage to start this innovation?

Feb. 14, 1954

Japan celebrated "Founding of the Nation Day" on the eleventh. Since this date is based on Shinto tradition, some other religions, especially Christianity, oppose the Shinto emphasis and some Christian churches joined in celebrating it unofficially as their own "Freedom of Religion" day, refusing to join in a Shinto celebration they claim is tied to the myth of the divine origin of Japan as a nation and the militaristic imperialism of the emperor system. A similar problem occurs when the emperor's birthday is celebrated April 29th. There is no such objection to the celebration of Constitution Day which occurs on May 3rd.

Fortunately, the celebration of Valentine's Day does not create much controversy. Last night we observed it by inviting over two recently married couples plus Tsuyuki-sensei, the new young pastor at Tomioka. We matched him up with Shigeko-san to make another couple for the party games. One of the games we devised was to put mixed letters of the alphabet in paper bags and then have each couple draw out individual letters in turn until some couple spells the word "love." To our amazement, the unmarried couple of Tsuyuki-sensei and Shigeko-san won three times out of five attempts.

After refreshments of cake, ice cream and nuts we closed the party with a hymn sing using both English and Japanese hymns. This morning I asked Shigeko-san if she was interested in Tsuyuki-sensei. She smiled shyly but quickly mentioned that it wouldn't work out since both he and she are the only child in their family. This means she must marry someone her folks can adopt to carry on the family name and Tsuyuki must seek a marriage arrangement that will allow him to carry on his family name. So much for our attempt at matchmaking.

To outdo Edward, Mary vomited up a six-inch stomach round worm. Lillian mentioned this at her woman's meeting and one lady said her young son had vomited up six. We gave Mary the cure right away but she got very nauseous, so it is probably too strong for her one-year old stomach. Kids seem to get these parasites from playing outside in contaminated dirt.

Feb. 23, 1954

Yesterday I went with Lillian to Kyoto for her language exam on the first book of the Naganuma Series. I knew what she was in for since I've taken exams all the way up to Book III—having had more opportunities for study than she has had. Hayashi-sensei had her write for two hours before lunch just on the first part of the book. There was a lunch break and then she wrote for two more hours on the second part. At three, just as a day-long snowstorm was ending, one teacher quizzed her on the contents of the book while two others sat behind her and wrote down all her errors. She passed the conversation part, did fairly well on the written parts but needs to work on her grammar.

Kyoto was spared bomb damage during the war but the train station burned down just before we arrived in Japan. The new station is beautiful with a very fine restaurant and a large shopping center where you can buy almost anything. We bought some gifts for the children then went on to Osaka where we visited with Alice Grube and Henry Jones until eleven, arriving home at midnight. Henry is our newest missionary, specializing in industrial evangelism after long experience in this field in Detroit, Michigan.

March 7, 1954

Lillian is losing one of her assistant teachers in the Sunday school in Nagano because she is starting work in a beauty parlor in a department store and has to work on Sunday. All the department stores do their biggest business on Sunday. Most factories are closed then as well as other businesses so people are free to shop and enjoy themselves. Only Christians go to religious services Sunday morning. Japanese traditional religious services are limited to certain dates which may fall on any day of the week depending on the year; however, some of the new religious, such as Tenrikyo and Soka Gakkai have daily services in temples or home, usually early morning or late evening, before or after work. Our weekly schedule is:

	Larry	Lillian	House
Sunday	1. Yao church 2. Nagano 3. Izumi-Sano 4. Tondabayashi	1. Sunday school 2. 10:00 church 3. teachers' meeting	meals, children, beds
Monday	house repairs, recreation, reading	language study	washing, meals, children
Tuesday	a.m.— study p.m.— guests, open house	housework, guests, study	ironing, children, meals
Wednesday	a.m.— study p.m.— Bible class	school, language class, children	sewing, meals, children
Thursday	school, study with teacher, prayer meeting	housework, children, study	cleaning, meals, children
Friday	a.m.— study p.m.— Bible class, language class, special meeting	school, language class, children	shopping, clean kitchen, meals, children
Saturday	dentist in Osaka, language class, Sunday preparation	dentist in Osaka, language class, Sunday preparation	cleaning, baking, meals, children

Shigeko-san and Lillian both cried during devotions Friday night, it being Shigeko-san's last night with us. The new girl, Debbie Ikuhashi, is good in English but knows little about housework. Lillian has to teach her everything which puts an extra burden on her until she learns. Edward lost his dinner during the night last night. It seems to be related to the loss of Shigeko-san.

March 14, 1954
Our school is preparing for new students to enter the first of April when all schools begin. Graduation exercises are next week. Their summer vacation lasts for a month and a half. Nagano has public school up through junior high but students must go to Tondabayashi for high school which is one reason our school wants to move on from junior high to senior high as soon as possible.

The $1,000 we requested from Second Church in Baltimore, where Lillian served as D.R.E., didn't come through so we have agreed to liquidate our savings in America to help relocate the nursery school which is being forced out by the rival secular school. Lillian has been chosen as the new head of the nursery as no appropriate Japanese director could be found, mainly because of rivalry among possible candidates claims Pastor Hashimoto.

With Debbie providing limited help I cooked Lillian's birthday dinner on the ninth. We had roast chicken (no dressing!), baked potatoes, carrots and peas, gravy, ice cream, cake, coffee and peanuts. Lillian graciously said, "It was as good as any dinner we could have bought in a restaurant."

Shigeko-san was our invited guest and kindly agreed to come a bit early to make an icing for the cake which I wasn't sure how to do. Lillian didn't know she was coming and Edward almost gave away the surprise when he suddenly asked "Where is Shigeko-san?" Lillian began to catch on when she saw an extra plate set at the table and was overjoyed when Shigeko-san walked in. I had piled up several presents at Lillian's plate.

One thing she wanted was underwear. A man would never buy such a thing in Japan so again I solved the problem by depending on faithful Shigeko-san. I kept Lillian guessing for a long time as to who had bought it. Debbie gave her a blue scarf and Shigeko-san gave a lovely Bambi figurine. Just as we were eating, a package from Mother Cassel arrived with more goodies, expert timing for overseas mail. Lillian's favorite in the box was thin chocolate mints and Edward's was fig newtons, neither of which we have been able to find in Japan. I was happy with the several kinds of cheese included.

Afterward Lillian and I saw *The Charge of the Light Brigade* at our small local movie house while the girls cleaned up. The movie house was unheated and, although the movie was interesting, we were glad to get back to a warm house. Enjoying her day off, Lillian sat up until midnight reading poetry. Lillian was born on her mother's birthday so it is a little sad not being able to celebrate together as they did for so many years before we came to Japan.

We usually end our nightly devotions with the Lord's Prayer after which Edward is allowed to take a *mikan* from the refrigerator and eat it before going to bed. Recently Lillian was listening to a religious radio program during the day which ended with someone saying the Lord's Prayer. As soon as they said amen, Edward ran to the refrigerator for a *mikan*.

March 22, 1954

Debbie Ikuhashi is gradually learning how to do things, but it is increasingly apparent that her main object is to learn English conversation, not do housework. We usually put Mary to bed in her pajamas at seven. Last night Debbie put her to bed at six with all her clothes on, just as we do for her daytime nap. Mary was taking it all without a whimper wondering what was going on. Knowing she was not sleepy. Lillian let her get up and run around again until seven.

Japanese artisans make a type of wooden doll that varies according to the district they are from. One type shows a mother carrying her baby on her back, according to local custom. When we sent some of these dolls to friends in America we got two interesting reactions. One person wanted to know if these were the kinds of idols the Japanese worshipped, another wanted to know why one doll had a tiny head sticking out of its back (it symbolized a mother carrying a baby). Cross-cultural communication can be difficult and confusing. In Japanese the dolls are called *kokeshi ningyo.*

In response to another question from American friends we made the following analysis of our Japanese address: Japan, Osaka State, (called fu or ken), Minami Kawachi County (called gun), Nagano Town (called cho or machi), 335 Furuno Block (called chome). In American style it would be: 335 Old Field Block, Long Field Town, South Inner-River County, Big Slope (Hill) State, Japan. The big difference is that the house has a block number instead of a street number.

March 28, 1954

Friday we had just returned from a long day in Wakayama City when I was called to a special meeting at the city hall concerning the nursery school competition from the secular group that is trying to push us out. The meeting began at seven and went on until three in the morning! It looks like we will be forced to move since too many secular political powers are arrayed against us. Nagano church members feel they are being oppressed unjustly.

However, there are encouraging things happening also. Five new students have begun attending our Sunday school through the influence of Edward and Mary—their playmates in the community. Then two of the four boys from my Tondabayashi Bible class who were baptized at Christmas just told me that they plan to become Christian pastors. Matsudasan, a dedicated Christian widow, is busy saving money to send her oldest son to seminary.

It looks like Tondabayashi church will be able to call a pastor! Some good friends from the Westminster Foundation at Penn State have offered monthly support to make this possible. The church expects to be able to pay the entire salary in a year and then the outside support could be used elsewhere.

The March wind was so strong today it blew open our front door and broke three glass panes in the door between the hall and the kitchen. Fortunately no one was hurt by the flying glass.

Lillian's mother asked us to identify the ending on Japanese names. Of course it could be confusing to outsiders as *sensei* means teacher, *san* simply indicates an adult and *chan* a child. *Kun* is an informal name ending for boys and men with whom one is very familiar. For a woman who is married the term is *okusan*, meaning the "one inside the house." *Oniisan* means older brother and *onaysan* older sister. A waitress in a restaurant is also called *onaysan* (sister). *Obasan* is aunt, and *obahsan* is grandmother. *Ojisan* is uncle and *ojiisan* is grandfather. Since we hear these terms almost every day we get used to them very soon. I forgot, *otooto* means younger brother and *imooto* means younger sister. *Anata* is a polite term for you as opposed to *omae*, a derogatory form of you.

April 5, 1954

Thursday was the big day of Nakayama-sensei's wedding. He is the founder of our school who sold his family home to help finance its beginning and is also an elder in Nagano church who never fails to tithe to the church even when his school is in financial danger. He is one of the finest Christians I have met anywhere. He came home from the war sick with typhus fever and almost died. He was in bed for a year and during that time an old school friend, Tsujino-sensei, brought him a Bible which he read through several times and was converted. As a Sunday school teacher he felt that more than one hour a week was needed to train young leaders of the new Japan to avoid mistakes like the aggressive war in Asia, culminating in Pearl Harbor and Japan's eventual defeat. He felt he was lied to many times by the military and he never wanted the military to control Japan again, so he started the school by building a shed room on the side of his home, inviting students from his public school classes to come at night for free tutoring in any subject he could help with. His fine Christian spirit and sacrificial way of life led others to support his efforts and Seikyo Gakuen (Puritan School) was born.

Lillian helped prepare food for the wedding feast. The chief item was *osushi* which the ladies prepare by cutting up mushrooms, green beans and bamboo sprouts into tiny pieces and then mix it into rice in huge wooden bowls. The mixture is put into individual wooden boxes and topped with peas, fried egg cut into thin strips and colorful decorative red ginger strips. A wooden lid is placed on each box which is then wrapped in white paper with a red carp design (symbolizing virility, since the carp swims upstream). Chopsticks are added and a rubber band holds it all secure until it is served to the wedding guests.

The wedding was Western style, except for the "go-between" couple who took the place of the parents and attendants. Lately we've noticed that the custom of having a best man and a maid of honor are gradually becoming popular. There were about 120 people present and the wedding and reception lasted for four hours. Everyone had coffee, tea and cookies but the *osushi* boxes were limited to the wedding party and honored guests, which included about half the crowd! Not only were pictures taken of the bride and groom and wedding party but many group pictures also—school friends, church friends, the women's association, et al. It was a happy, but exhausting experience.

Yesterday Captain Mitsuo Fuchida, the leader of the air force squadron that bombed Pearl Harbor, spoke for over an hour to our Kaizuka group. He was converted through the evangelistic efforts of one of the Doolittle flyers, Mr. Jacob Deshazer, and has distributed scriptures for the Pocket Testament League throughout Japan for the past four years. In 1950 he began as the driver, interpreter and assistant to Rev. George Vorsheim of our Presbyterian church and together they distributed a quarter million Gospels of John in Japan's northern Island of Hokkaido.

When Vorsheim asked him what he was thinking when he

was bombing ships and sailors at Pearl Harbor he answered, "I couldn't see the men and I felt I was doing a good job—the job I was assigned to do. I had been taught that Americans were torturing our prisoners of war so I was glad to hurt them back."

"What do you think of America now?" Vorsheim quizzed.

"Now that I know more about it, I think it is the greatest country in the world, a leader in democracy."

After the Sunday evening meeting Capt. Fuchida returned with us and spent the night as our guest. Lillian was pleasantly surprised to find she understood most of his talk to the Kaizuka people.

A few nationalistic Japanese resent such a war hero becoming a Christian and try to oppose him. I wonder if that is why he keeps his home guarded with two fierce German shepherd police dogs whom I had to face when I visited his home in Nara to invite him to witness for us. A visiting pastor was bitten by one of them.

Fuchida is a great admirer of General Douglas MacArthur for his benevolent treatment of Japan after their defeat and for requesting the distribution of millions of gospel tracts in Japan. I marvel at how God can use even the military.

April 11, 1954

Edward started nursery school last Thursday and seems to like it. In fact he hates to come home to eat lunch with us as most of the kids eat at the school. However, we think half a day is enough for him and he needs to be home to hear more English spoken. Lillian is now teaching English classes at Seikyo Gakuen about three days a week, a few hours each day. Mary is just beginning to talk. I call her "Chubby Mary" and after I dressed her on Thursday and brought her down to breakfast she turned to Lillian and said "Chubby Mother." Naturally Lillian had mixed feelings about that.

Shoe repair is proving a problem in Nagano as they use such hard, inflexible leather for resoling it is hard to walk in repaired shoes. We may try the larger repair shops in Osaka.

Dealers in leather and slaughter house workers are all considered "outcasts" in Japan. This apparently stems from the influx of Buddhism with its prohibition of killing animals. Many people eat meat and use leather but those who prepare these items are considered ritually "unclean." Originally called *Eta* they are now called *Buraku-bito* (village people or ghetto-dwellers). They look the same as other Japanese and the postwar law is that they should not be discriminated against, but it still occurs.

I know one "outcast" girl who secretly married outsiders twice but her marriage was annulled each time, immediately when it was discovered she originally came from an outcast village. Koreans also have a hard time in Japan, although the situation is improving. Koreans were brought over by force to work in Japan's war industry and yet they are not fully accepted. They complain that they must be fingerprinted like criminals and carry a foreign registration card all the time. We missionaries also have to do this but it is common knowledge that Japan's fingerprinting is aimed chiefly at Koreans who resent Japan's domination and are suspected of being sympathetic with Communist North Korea.

April 25, 1954

On Thursdays I now teach three English classes at Seikyo Gakuen School and Lillian teaches two on Wednesday and one on Friday. She is teaching the kindergarteners their ABCs and has two classes of a hundred each. She makes a game of it, teaching them to sing the ABC song and using visual aids. For English conversation classes in the junior high we manage to get the classes down to 20 but that is still too large. Time limitations do not permit us to teach more classes. English grammar and composition are taught by a Japanese teacher.

A train strike prevented me from going to Nara to preach today. At 5:30 p.m. I went by car to Kaizuka as the strike was still on.

Yesterday we did our monthly shopping in Osaka and then took Edward and Mary to the zoo. There were a great many bears (in Hokkaido the Ainu aboriginal people treat the bear as sacred). The Ainu kill bears for food but do it with a religious ceremony to placate the bear's spirit. At the zoo the animals we missed were elephants and giraffes. Large animals like this were destroyed during the war and have not yet been replaced, but smaller animals abound.

Our biggest surprise was to find a harlequin block of delicious ice cream being sold at the snack shops. Good ice cream is just appearing in Japan, made by Hokkaido dairies which also make good cheese. At 18 months Mary walked better than three-year-old Edward who alternated between wanting a drink or wanting to sit down.

April 29, 1954 — Easter

At our Easter service in Nagano today four graduates of our school were baptized along with an older girl who is assisting as a teacher in Sunday school. Two of the boys were sons of elders in the church. This is a welcome change as the usual pattern is that the baptized person is the only Christian in the family—which complicates things as one then comes into conflict with the traditional religions of Shinto and Buddhism which control life from birth to death for most Japanese.

The saying is, "The Shinto shrine marries you and the Buddhist temple buries you." There are few burial places outside a temple. Christian churches are being forced to build mausoleums to have a place to bury Christians. It is difficult to become a Christian when one knows it will bring dissension with Shinto and Buddhist relatives and friends. Pastor Hashimoto prepares baptismal candidates well and, with church support, most of them live a dedicated and courageous Christian life, putting many of us to shame.

Today Sunday school began at eight, followed by the worship service and a congregational meeting which lasted until five. Lillian said it was quite a test of her ability to survive long meetings in Japanese. At the Nagano church we have 88 members but only half were able to be at the congregational meeting and that number had dwindled to 21 by the time of the closing prayer. Elders were elected by having everyone present write the names of those they wanted as elders on a piece of paper. These were collected and the results were collated on a blackboard with everyone looking on.

To acquaint Edward and Mary with American Easter customs we hid two Easter baskets of colored eggs and candies and let them find them at home. Churches here have not adopted this custom.

Tondabayashi church now has its first full-time pastor. Pastors Hashimoto, Tsuyuki, Lillian and I ate a crab feast with him at an elder's home last night. Later we ate again at a reception at the church. The new pastor is a good friend of young Pastor Tsuyuki at Tomioka and we like him very much. Both of them are graduates of Biblical Seminary in Tokyo—which conducts most of its classes at night as the students have to work in the daytime to pay for their education. The new pastor is quite energetic and intense, much more of an extrovert than most Japanese people. Pastor Tsuyuki is an introvert type and Pastor Hashimoto is between the other two. Any day now we will probably be forming a ministerial fellowship for our area.

May 2, 1954

A month ago the police came and asked us to bring our driver's licenses to the primary school on a certain day to have our address changed. Since I had to be in Tokyo that day Lillian took them. Lillian wrote her mother the following description: "I showed them to some man (goodness knows whom!) but he just looked at them and thanked me. When I insisted that he do something, he just said it was all right. So I returned home and told Larry when he came back from Tokyo. Yesterday we got a notice asking us to come to Osaka because we had not followed the instructions here to have our licenses changed! Larry spent the whole lunch time lecturing me on the mistake I made in not taking a Japanese person with me, and then we went to the local police station where he lectured them on allowing such a thing to happen. Fortunately they are our friends and have agreed to accept the responsibility of going to Osaka on our behalf.

"We still don't know what happened. But Larry is always so afraid we are going to get into trouble with the authorities and be sent home, or just create bad feeling for the church or America. We do have to bend over backwards to be careful, especially when there is so much anti-American feeling in Japan now. We were both exhausted last night and I think the tenseness of the situation was what tired us."

This is just one example of the extra strain on people living and working in a different nation and culture. Today a train strike had me chauffeuring people from Yao to Tondabayashi, to Nagano, to Tomioka for an area meeting of pastors and elders in the afternoon. Then I drove back to Nagano and on to Kaizuka for a late evening meeting. Such is the life of a missionary, demanding but rewarding. The Tomioka meeting was to plan a unified mission effort of cooperation and mutual support for the whole area, called "Kanan Mission."

Kitano-sensei, the lady assistant to Pastor Hashimoto, works too hard partly because she fears other Sunday school teachers are not "qualified." We are trying to help by doing a lot of teacher training. Lillian is a big help as she works directly with the teachers at Nagano church every Sunday.

Seeing that the children who came early were at loose ends, Lillian started a junior choir for them. Today was their first practice and every teacher showed up early to see what was going on. With all that interest and talent I don't think Kitano-sensei needs to worry so about getting the job done and can soon learn to trust others to help her carry the ball.

May 9, 1954—Mother's Day

Japan does not celebrate Mother's Day as we do in the States but the Christian churches are beginning to follow the American custom, including the wearing of red or white flowers to honor one's mother. I bought red carnations for all of us to wear to church today but Mary kept taking hers off to play with it.

Japanese footwear customs continue to intrigue us. Wednesday we went to visit friends in Chiyoda, an adjoining town, and when we went walking in the garden the hostess provided wooden *geta* for each of us to slip into quickly instead of having to bother with shoes. We always have to take off our shoes when we go into any house, the local churches or our school. Some city churches and schools are beginning to build buildings of concrete with floors designed for shoes, as do department stores and some public buildings in big cities. We like the new convenience.

May 17, 1954

The three churches of Nagano, Tomioka and Tondabayashi had a joint picnic yesterday which was a lot of fun. We had the worship service on a mountain top in Tondabayashi at eleven followed by a picnic lunch and a business meeting. After that we had softball competition between the three churches. Tomioka church beat Tondabayashi and then Tondabayashi played Nagano. I played for Nagano and Nakayama-sensei and I both got home runs to tie the score. At that critical juncture we had to leave as I had an evening meeting in Kaizuka, so we still don't know who came out as champion of the three churches. Nagano, as the largest group, probably will have won.

Shigeko-san does not seem to be happy staying home all the time so we are offering to take her for an outing in Kyoto as we go to see Dr. Alice Cary there next Monday. Even though technically Shigeko-san is an "annullee" she is treated as a young divorcee here in Japan which puts her in an awkward social position.

Since she is a good seamstress Lillian is considering employing her to make the curtains and slip covers we need, which could lead to other seamstress jobs for her once it becomes known that even the foreigners in town think she is good enough to employ.

Saturday Lillian went to Nara-ken to speak to the women in the Gose church and Pastor Tokita went along to escort her on the train since I was away at another meeting. She said they barely made the train going, and even then Tokita ran ahead to hold the train. Coming back they were late finishing up the cooking class Lillian gave which stressed nutrition and meal planning but which she topped off with making a dish of peas in white sauce. To make the train Pastor Tokita put Lillian on the back of his bicycle and pedaled furiously over the bumpy roads with Lillian hanging on for dear life over each bump. Thankfully they made the train and Lillian arrived home safely, a little shaken up but still in one piece.

May 23, 1954

Two recent incidents have reinforced for us how often Japanese customs differ from ours. Our friend Midori Yamamoto and her husband are having a disagreement about their living situation because she wants a place of their own while he insists they must live with his folks, according to the Japanese custom, since he can't afford a separate home. This is a serious problem in Japan since the daughter-in-law is expected to serve her mother-in-law, almost like a servant, and many young brides are rebelling. Recently a family we know sent their daughter back when she ran away from the in-law's home and she committed suicide by drinking poison.

The other experience had to do with the Japanese custom of being less concerned about supervising children constantly than we are. The other day Lillian took Edward to nursery school and found a dozen children there with no teacher. She waited an hour, then discovered both teachers were late because they wanted first shot at buying clothes at our church bazaar and felt the children would be fine until they got there.

Incidentally, the bazaar is a commercial venture of Japanese business people who buy American used clothing and offer our churches eight percent of the sales price for sponsoring the bazaar in the church facilities. Although Japan is recovering well from the losses of the war, clothing is still scarce and expensive so this type of used clothing sale is popular. When the customer finds what they want they take the item to the door where it is wrapped in newspaper and the money paid to the volunteers from our women's association. Crowds came in the morning to get the best pick but few came in the afternoon. Lillian helped most of the day and wore her official badge, just like the others.

Edward speaks both English and Japanese but refuses to speak English to a Japanese person or Japanese to Americans. Mary is learning both languages by imitating Edward. Japanese doctors give so many shots for whatever ails you that Edward is getting used to that too. About a week ago he had an upset stomach with fever and when the doctor gave him the usual shot he acted like it was no big deal. Typhoid immunizations and measles shots are important here as they are common, but there is no shot for Edward's latest problem—he collided with a boy at nursery school and got a front tooth knocked out which makes him look like "Peck's bad boy."

May 26, 1954

Our Tuesday open house is proving almost too popular. In the morning Pastor Tokita sent two of his church women to observe Western living and learn cooking. They stayed all day! Usually guests stay only an hour or two so we don't have to serve them a meal but these ladies joined us for lunch and informed us that two women would be coming at least once a month from now on.

Nakayama-sensei brought over 40 students from the school and Lillian was so tired she had to greet them upstairs in her housecoat. Two others came and brought a Japanese doll but they didn't stay as there were so many here. One brilliant young boy seems interested in becoming a Christian.

All these guests are a great strain on Lillian and, to make matters worse, we just learned from Dr. Alice Cary that she is low on iron and also needs to resume taking thyroid. Lillian's weight has dropped from 128 pounds to 114 and she stays exhausted much of the time and has many colds.

We have another meeting of our nursery school board members tonight but Lillian isn't well enough to make it. Dr.

Cary was low on her supply of iron and thyroid pills so we had to write Lillian's mother to send some from America. Dr. Cary joked with Lillian suggesting a sure way of getting sent home early on furlough would be to get pregnant because with our Rh negative factor, the mission would not want us to risk another birth in Japan.

May 30, 1954

The new mayor of Kawachi-Nagano-Shi (the current name of our city since it is now updated from a town) is friendly to us and we believe that he will help us come to some just solution on the nursery school controversy with the secular group. The last meeting he moderated between the opposing groups lasted only two hours instead of the five to ten hours we have had in the past.

We celebrated our fifth wedding anniversary this week by a visit to Osaka Prefecture Fair with exhibits, rides and wild animal shows just like an American circus. For our dinner we had a luscious hamburger, coffee (bitter as could be) and a deluxe sundae, which still doesn't come up to our banana splits. My culinary fantasy is to come home and have alternate meals of hamburgers and banana splits and hamburgers and chocolate milk shakes. Afterwards we went to see "Beneath the Twelve Mile Reef" in cinema-scope and found it almost too exciting, for it was difficult to relax with so much going on at once.

Grace Hessel still has dinner with us every Thursday, after teaching music at our school, and she gave us a wooden doll (*Kokeshi Ningyo*) for an anniversary present since this is the "wood" anniversary.

Tomorrow we have to get our regular X-rays for T.B. Since practically everyone here seems to get it sooner or later, that is what we have to watch for all the time.

June 6, 1954

The rainy season, plus a busy schedule, makes us all sleepy. Today I left early for Yao where I had Sunday school, worship and lunch and then arrived back in Nagano for an early afternoon mission committee meeting. After a quick bite of supper with the family I was off to Kaizuka for the evening service and then got home at eleven.

Tuesday we had ten ministers at our home for an all day meeting. Lillian served everyone dinner at noon time and tea at four. The children ate a picnic lunch outside (which they preferred) as we didn't have room at the table for them.

On Wednesday both children ran high fevers as a result of their typhoid shots this week. Thursday they were better so tomorrow it looks like we can take them back for their final shots in the series. On our chest X-rays taken by Dr. Sawada, mine showed scars from a possible T.B. infection but I seemed to be fine now. The rest of the family showed no problem.

Friday we had 24 women and eight children here for the women's association meeting. The new pastor at Tondabaya-shi gave a talk after which there was a short business meeting. Lillian served strawberry shortcake with whipped cream but the evaporated milk didn't whip so she was very disappoint-ed. The women didn't know what was hoped for and they thought it was delicious with just the cream poured over it. Afterward the women wanted to see our snapshot albums.

After bowing to all the women coming in and to most of them leaving, Lillian confessed to the remaining women that her back was killing her from so much bowing. They got quite a laugh out of it and one of the women gave her a rub-down. We are finally getting to know them well enough to joke with them in this way. One lady said Japanese ladies often bow five to ten times when once or twice is sufficient! Maybe Lillian is overdoing it a bit.

The United Church of Christ (Kyodan) missionaries want to have their own fellowship (in addition to the broader ecumenical one) and it is up to me as English secretary of the Cooperative Evangelism Council (CEC) to set it up for the first time. We drew names out of a hat for the food everyone is to bring according to a planned menu. So far everyone is expecting to come except one, but Lillian will have to make two dishes to make up for the missing person. She said she hopes no one else has to cancel out so she doesn't have to cook three dishes.

June 13, 1954

It took us three hours to get to the missionary outing yesterday but the beautiful scenery and good fellowship made it worthwhile. We even had enough people for an interesting softball game. Lillian is exhausted from spring cleaning plus entertaining so many guests recently and has had to refuse persistent requests from the women of Gose church in Nara Prefecture because she doesn't feel up to the long trip there plus the speaking and teaching cooking as she did earlier. They have asked her to come three times and don't seem to take "no" for an answer. Lillian is desperately in need of a vacation. Fortunately she will get one at Lake Nojiri soon. Iron and thyroid pills do help her feel better.

The nursery school struggle with the secular group has moved to the Osaka Prefectural level where the secular group feels they have power enough to push out the Christian group. Endless trips to the prefectural offices in Osaka are exhausting all of us. With money, political power and persistence the secular group may yet get their own way, even though our local mayor sides with us.

June 20, 1954

Buying meat is an adventure in Japan. Lillian has tried to get our local butchers to give her cuts similar to those we get in the States but they find that difficult to do. Yet it always tastes good so we eat it without complaint. Beef costs about three times what it does in America and ham is even higher and then only available in big cities like Osaka. For some reason beef liver is very reasonable, probably because the Japanese don't like it much so we have it about once a week. Chicken and fish are available anytime at reasonable prices.

Father's Day has been turned into Children's Day by our local Nagano church and they showed the children two *Kami-*

shibai (like our flannelgraph stories told with large pictures on cardboard). The various pictures are displayed, one on top of the other, until the set is complete. Accompanying this is a tape recording of the story told with special sound effects. A few professional storytellers gather children on the streets and narrate children's stories after which they sell candy or ice cream to the kids to make a living. We see them even in small towns and cities like ours.

Lillian is hoping to get our Sunday school children involved in more hand work, rather than being taught by the lecture method so much.

Shigeko-san came by to tell us that her peritonitis has flared up again. She also informed us that our old landlord's son, Tadayoshi Hayakawa, has been operated on for appendicitis. Tadayoshi's favorite dog, Tenryu (dragon), died and got a first class funeral, but they are keeping this quiet so outsiders will not know their good watch dog is dead. In fact he was such a good watch dog that he bit me once, even though he knew I lived next door.

When we went to make a sick call on Tadayoshi we saw Mrs. Hayakawa's brother's new baby daughter who is just five months old—a real doll. Tadayoshi's father told us the spinal block anesthetic they used for Tadayoshi's operation did not work well so he was in tremendous pain.

Shigeko-san also told us her good friend Mrs. Fujita, who married one of our school teachers, has pleurisy. The Fujitas had waited three years to marry because of poor health for both of them. Now having become pregnant seems to have brought back some of her earlier problems, although the baby seems to be fine. At least Mr. Fujita's T.B. is cured.

June 27, 1954

With the weather so hot and muggy during this rainy season almost everyone feels the need of a little "siesta" after lunch. Japanese workers are accustomed to a tea break in mid morning and mid afternoon, but only those who don't have a public job can take naps after lunch. Every time we have repair people come to work on our house or our car we have to serve them tea. Even delivery people bringing heavy objects such as furniture to the house expect tea to be served them and it is considered rude not to provide it. We try to follow these customs as closely as we can as we want to show our respect for Japanese customs.

Lillian is looking forward to our vacation at cool Lake Nojiri and so is Edward who remembers the good swimming there. Monday we went into Osaka to shop and bought some toys for sand and water for Edward and Mary to use at Nojiri. That really got Edward excited. While Lillian was buying some shoes and doing birthday shopping for her dad, I took Mary and Edward to the playground on the roof of the Sogo Department Store. Every department store tries to provide such a play area for children with swings and slides in an atmosphere of green plants and flowers growing. This seems to be such a good idea for older children can take care of younger ones there while their parents shop.

Debbie, our new helper, says her mother wants her to be a secretary but she wants to write poetry or paint. She is not a bit business-like so her mother's wishes seem a bit unrealistic. On the other hand she is attractive, has a beautiful voice and speaks English well which might enable her to get a job on television or radio, or as an interpreter or travel guide. We do hope she can use her natural talent somewhere.

One day Debbie told me I had T.B. Apparently she had heard of the scar tissue that showed up on one of my X-rays. I patiently explained that while I was exposed to T.B. my lungs were now clear and I did not have it. She insisted that I did, which got us into quite an argument. I was getting quite irritated with her when she suddenly smiled and said, "Yes, I know. But today is my day to study argument."

Life is never dull with Debbie around.

July 4, 1954

Lillian didn't realize what day it was until I greeted her with "Happy Fourth of July." She tried to explain its meaning to Edward but he is just too young to take it all in. At the moment he is upstairs entertaining Mary with some of his antics, which must be funny since Mary is laughing hilariously.

The rainy season has resulted in heavy flooding in Osaka Prefecture and also in Wakayama. We bought an American-made sofa and chair from Grace Hessel for our living room, but they can't be delivered until the flood waters go down. We decided on used furniture because the kids would wreck new Japanese furniture, which is not built to withstand the use of heavy Westerners.

Wednesday when I drove to Tondabayashi for my Bible class a long section of road was flooded. Lillian and Edward went along to visit Shigeko-san's friend, Mrs. Fujita, who has been so ill but is now all right so she can return to her husband's family home. When a wife gets sick here and is considered unable to work for her husband and his family, she usually returns to her parents to be cared for, while the husband continues to live with his family. Since she can work again, she can return to her husband's family to serve them.

Wednesday Lillian and I will go to Osaka to buy our tickets for Lake Nojiri. Japanese regulations do not allow tickets to be bought more then a week ahead and if you wait to the last moment you may not be able to get a seat. Lillian, the children and Debbie will go on ahead and then I will join them after a two-week evangelistic tour of Wakayama Prefecture. Since Matsuda-san, the widow with four children, has no home of her own she will stay in our house as *rusuban* (house watcher) while we are away on vacation.

The Hashimotos are in their new house and love it. We took a gift of fruit over to them on Wednesday.

Today I finally got to dictate a letter for Debbie to write in Japanese notifying the caretaker of cabins in Nojiri that we would be coming soon and to please open and clean it. I also requested that he put up pipes from the roof to the water tank to collect water for washing dishes and clothing. We carry all our drinking water from a fresh water spring down by the lake, a quarter mile away, where water gushes out from a steep hill and is cold and delicious.

July 11, 1985

Although the travel bureau was jammed we managed to get tickets to Nojiri. Lillian, Debbie and the kids will stay overnight in Osaka with Alice Grube in order to get an early morning train Wednesday. They have to change at Nagoya and wait an hour for a connection to Nagano City in the mountain country where they'll arrive in the evening and spend the night at a hotel there where they have a reservation. Thursday they will ride three more hours to get to Nojiri by way of Kashiwabara, arriving about noon to get settled in the cabin before nightfall.

Edward seems a bit accident prone. In addition to falling out the second story window at nine months of age, he fell out of a boat at Nojiri last summer. Today he swallowed a big black button from a "Go" game and fell through the glass door of the living room for a second time. He was bouncing on the springs of our couch and propelled himself through the glass door into the hall, with only a small bit of glass stuck in his head to show for it. By the time Lillian had put iodine and a bandage on him he looked like a wounded veteran.

Earlier he had gotten the key down from a nail on the wall to let himself out to play in the yard after Lillian had locked him in so she could get a much needed nap. We can never relax entirely with Edward, Mary and Debbie around.

Aug. 8, 1954

After two weeks away from the family it was good to join them at Nojiri Lake. Together we are enjoying swimming, relaxing and the great summer vegetables available here—corn on the cob, summer squash and rhubarb pie. Trying to catch up too fast with the tennis, golf and hiking, I fell and cut my knee which gives me something in common with Edward's sore toe. Lillian says he kept asking "Where is Daddy?" the entire two weeks I was away from them.

Mary got upset Sunday morning when we didn't go for

our usual morning swim. Since we swim every other morning she just couldn't understand why not this day. Later she disappeared, apparently having decided she was going swimming whether we did or not. After a frantic half hour, we found her wandering down one of the narrow trails to the lake, a very dangerous thing for a two-year-old to do. Fortunately, she had not reached the lake for she would probably have jumped in for a "swim," her favorite pastime.

Aug. 23, 1954

About 400 people attended the Fellowship of Christian Missionaries conference here at Lake Nojiri. One of the high points of the summer for me was getting to know Dr. Emil Brunner and hearing him speak here several times. Hearing that Japanese Christians are strict about not smoking or drinking he gave up smoking during his several months in Japan. I admire him for that.

Friday Lillian and I went hiking to a nearby waterfall with Dick and Pearl Drummond. We left early, ate lunch at the falls and got back after three. At the falls Lillian slipped on the rocks in the stream and fell in up to her thighs. She scrambled out and said the numbingly cold water which comes from snow melt made it feel like sinking into quick sand. Last summer the heavy rains brought flooding so high no one could even get close enough to see the falls. This year Dick and I were able to go and stand right under them—a wet, misty thrill.

Other highlights of the summer at Nojiri were the annual picnic with several hundred fellow missionaries on the golf course and the weekly hymn sings out on the lake in boats. We usually rowed out in our boat but one Sunday we were invited to tie our boat on to a friend's motor boat so got a free ride, touring the inlets of the lake before the hymn sing began. Edward loved this special treat.

Since Debbie got into poison ivy, Lillian has had to do most of the dish washing and laundry.

Sept. 5, 1954

Our trip home was not too bad. Closing up the cabin took until two Wednesday afternoon then we left by train for Nagano City where we spent the night in a hotel. After a Japanese-style hot bath for all of us, we enjoyed a sukiyaki dinner. When the children were ready for bed Lillian and I left them in Debbie's care and went to see the movie "Julius Caesar" which was playing at a nearby theater.

After a good Western-style breakfast of bacon and eggs we boarded a third class train the next morning which got us to Nagoya by late afternoon. For lunch we bought the Japanese-style lunches sold in wooden lunch boxes at all major railway stations. The rice and vegetable *eki-bento* (station lunch) was quite tasty. We ate dinner in Nagoya where we had an hour to wait and then got on an express train which rushed us to Osaka in three hours. By that time Mary was tired of trains and we had to do a bit of persuading to get her on board. We crossed town in a a taxi to Namba station in plenty of time to line up for the nine o'clock express to Kawachi-Nagano.

Getting on that train was our only real difficulty. Each of us had all the luggage we could carry, including Edward with his own small bag. Just as we started to enter the train a whole gang of young fellows came rushing up and in their pushing to be the first on the train in order to make sure they got a seat, poor Edward was shoved aside and got lost for a minute. When he started crying in a loud voice we located him and managed to get him aboard just as the train pulled out. While I was busy retrieving Edward, Lillian forgot her usual gentle ways and yelled at the young men to watch what they were doing. I have seldom seen her so angry or young men so chagrined as she scolded them in perfect *Naganuma Book I* style! We were mighty glad to be safely home by ten.

I was happy to find that most of the pictures I took of our two-week evangelistic tour of Wakayama Prefecture, just before vacation, turned out well. Three Doshisha Seminary students plus a local pastor had helped me to give two or three evangelistic presentations each day in the unchurched towns and villages there. We used a portable organ for much singing. A little preaching was included but our main evangelistic thrust was using puppets to present key Bible stories depicting God's love and forgiveness for all of us.

We arrived home from vacation three days ago, but our suitcases have not yet come. It is the custom in Japan to send the luggage by slower trains than the passengers usually ride, but they are good about sending luggage on to the nearest station and notifying us when to pick it up.

When we left on vacation Pastor Hashimoto's family was happily settling into their new home. Returning home we found they had another serious problem. With the extra expenses from moving in and trying to make-do on an inadequate income, they have not been eating enough nutritious food. The resulting vitamin and mineral deficiency caused the children to get painful boils all over their bodies. Five-year-old Mitsuru-chan's face is swollen and he has a fever.

I was relieved to hear that when the church became aware of the problem they, with great difficulty, increased his salary. Like most relatively affluent Americans we were shocked to come in such close contact with poverty. Worst of all was to hear that Mrs. Hashimoto, to get extra income, has taken up some poorly paying side work—stringing colored beads for Christmas tree decorations at a ridiculous wage of less than two cents an hour. It takes her an hour to string four sets and she gets only one yen per set. We have arranged for her to do some work for us at a much better wage. With the pastor's salary increase I believe the worst is over. We thought our budget was tight but it is luxurious compared to theirs.

This morning two more of Edward's playmates, living in back of us, appeared at Sunday school. He is indeed becoming our best missionary without even realizing it. God works in mysterious ways.

Evangelism has its difficulties now that the Japanese feel more free to criticize the State's weaknesses than they did after the war. At first this appeared detrimental to evangelism to me, but the more I thought about it, I realized this new-found freedom to talk about the good and the bad in the U.S. is a plus for evangelism. As one young man said, "We are not anti-American, we just feel free to say what we think now."

While we have been prevented from renting meeting places by two anti-Christian men in surrounding towns, we still have more opportunities for Christian meetings than we can possibly keep up with and all the new Christian groups that have been started here are growing slowly but steadily.

Sept. 20, 1954

In the last week we have had to make elaborate preparations when warned that typhoons No. 12 and 14 were headed our way. I nailed boards over all our windows—as did all our neighbors—but neither typhoon hit us directly. Last weekend No. 12 shook us up a bit with high winds and then drenched us with heavy rains, but no serious damage was done. Having lived through one which did damage our house earlier Lillian was frightened. Since I had escaped that experience, I found it easier to be fascinated by big natural upheavals like this.

Debbie's mother is not well and she tells us she must stop work to help her mother as soon as we can find someone to replace her. We will miss her, but she is really not suited for this type of work. Maybe later, when her mother is better, she can find something more appropriate.

Sept. 27, 1954

We are wondering if Lillian is pregnant again or is instead, at age 42, entering menopause. She feels a little nauseated, but colds have made most of the family feel a little upset, so that may not mean anything.

Saturday Pastor Hashimoto and I had to go to court with two Koreans, one of whom had gotten into trouble by buying stolen goods. Most Japanese people discriminate against Koreans—reminiscent of our own problems in the U.S. with racism. Lillian went along with us to Osaka and took Edward to the dentist. On our way home we all stopped at the Yao house church so Lillian could speak to the women. We all enjoyed their refreshments of hot tea served in glasses, rice balls covered with bean paste that looks like chocolate and is sweet, with others covered with a kind of orange icing, such as we put on cakes.

The Korean man was so grateful for us helping him out he did not complain about having to wait for Lillian.

Oct. 3, 1954

A sudden typhoon off the coast of Hokkaido sank the *Toyo Maru* killing two missionaries on their way to the same conference I attended in the Tokyo area. One of the ones lost was our good friend Alfred Stone, a Canadian missionary, who was active in rural evangelism and has visited here many times. We had just seen him this summer at Lake Nojiri. I remember him making a pun on his name and saying he could "swim like a Stone." However, an autopsy showed he did not die of drowning but was mercifully killed instantly by an object hitting him on the head.

An American missionary, Dean Leeper, was also killed. To prevent people going out into the high winds on deck the doors had been locked which prevented anyone from escaping to safety. One Canadian missionary, knocked unconscious, was washed out a porthole and woke up on the beach, not knowing how he got there. The only missionary saved, he says he will always wonder why he lived and others died.

Another missionary, Evyn Adams, was due to take the *Toyo Maru* but arrived too late to get on board so came to Tokyo by plane. When he arrived unexpectedly at a friend's home, they almost fainted, thinking it was his ghost! Everyone seems to be blaming the tragedy on the weather bureau for not warning the *Toyo Maru* about the coming of the typhoon. Their excuse was that they didn't know about it as they had no weather airplane to check the area. With no one to blame, and everyone to blame, no one would claim responsibility.

This morning we had another tragedy right near our house. An elderly lady jumped in front of a train between here and the Buddhist temple. Temples are often chosen as a place for suicides here. We woke up to see a crowd of people running past our house to the scene about 75 yards away where there have been three suicides there in recent years. Family problems and personal problems are usually the cause.

Today I spoke to four different church groups, in spite of having a cold. If this keeps up I will probably lose my voice and not be able to speak anywhere.

Oct. 10, 1954

Our local police complimented me with an invitation to speak to them last Monday on American police methods plus any thoughts I might have concerning police methods and philosophy in general. Pastor Hashimoto was supposed to meet me at the police station to act as interpreter; however he forgot and I was completely on my own. I made out fine as long as I stuck to explaining the American police system but the minute they started asking questions I was in trouble because they bombarded me with specialized police jargon which is not in my Japanese vocabulary.

Although I am fairly fluent in conversational Japanese and know church and theological terms I need more training in technical language for specialized fields. When I confessed my weakness in technical police terms the policemen very kindly explained their questions in simple lay person's language and I managed to get by.

The ideas hardest for them to accept were that even criminals deserve to be treated with respect and that there is always the possibility of rehabilitation for even hardened criminals. Their ideas seemed to be that once a person is found guilty they forfeit all rights to good treatment, mercy or forgiveness. Justice demands they be treated harshly as part of their punishment, the police claimed. The Christian idea of pardon is alien to them in this context. For them a criminal is a criminal, is a criminal, and deserves to be handled roughly.

Dr. Alice Cary has confirmed that Lillian is indeed pregnant and we are trying to determine what this means for our future plans. Lillian's idea is to ask Dr. Cary to let her go to

Tokyo to be under the care of Dr. Syphers who understands her Rh negative blood problem and could possibly save the baby. Dr. Cary seems to think we should go home early since we are due to go on furlough soon anyway and this would be much safer for the baby and for Lillian. We both feel that we are just becoming skilled enough in cross-cultural communication to do a good missionary job and would hate to go home early and lose a year of evangelistic opportunity.

Pastor Hashimoto has applied for a scholarship to study at a U.S. seminary and we hope he makes it. His English is good and we gave him a strong recommendation. The Nagano church tends to blame him for all their problems so it will be good if he can get away for a year to give everyone some perspective. I am sure the study will be good for all parties.

Oct. 26, 1954

Kaizuka has bought land for their own church building and has also saved up a good bit for the building. Last Sunday we planned to clean up the lot and have outdoor Sunday school and worship there, but it was rained out and we met in our rented quarters.

Debbie left us to help her mother last Wednesday but the lady who was supposed to replace her didn't show up. We later heard she had become ill and can't work for us. We have asked Pastor Hashimoto to help us find a good helper.

To add more confusion to the matter, three women from Osaka arrived at different times last week saying we had requested they come to interview for the job we had open for a helper. Apparently they were from a secular employment agency we would never think of using to find such an important person who will be responsible for the welfare of our children since we would have no way of checking their reliability. The mystery was solved when we discovered that Debbie, true to her unpredictable self, had requested the women to come for interviews without saying anything to us.

I guess she thought she was doing us a favor but it was embarrassing for us and the women who showed up unexpectedly. Good old Debbie! Who can forget that beautiful, un-organized, undependable, inscrutable young lady? We are keeping her as a friend but are glad not to have her unhappily fouling up the kitchen and our kids' thinking any more. Her dream is to marry a rich foreigner and, with her beauty and good English ability, she just might make it, providing he doesn't see through her charming scheme before it is too late. She wrote us saying "I have stopped going to church as depending on God makes me weak and I want to be strong." Living with her unhappy mother and her mother's contro-versial lover does not improve her prospects for the future.

Dr. Henry Jones was our guest from Friday to Sunday, providing leadership for an industrial evangelism emphasis at Kaizuka, a textile city with thousands of young girls who come from far away farms to run the machines that make all kinds of clothing. They live in company dormitories and send most of their earnings home to help relieve their parents' poverty. It seems cold-hearted to send the girls so far from home to work; however it is certainly better than the female infanticide, or selling girls to houses of prostitution, which was once a big problem in Japan.

With no helper for Lillian, who feels nauseated constantly, I am trying to assist around the house more in spite of almost daily church meetings in surrounding towns. We are both exhausted.

Edward's birthday on the 18th almost got lost in the rush, but we did work it out so he had ten children plus three mothers and Shigeko-san for a successful party. He was overjoyed to have his own party after having attended several for other kids at Nojiri. He really liked the record player Lillian and I gave him.

With Lillian not feeling well, I had to do all the food shopping as well as buy the gifts for the party. Lillian is taking sea-sick pills (dramamine) for her nausea and although this alleviates the nausea, it makes her very sleepy.

Oct. 31, 1954

My schedule is becoming really hectic and Lillian complains that she hardly ever sees me anymore. I am even more concerned that my constant absence will have adverse effects on our children. Edward especially seems to resent my being away so much. Mary, being younger, doesn't seem to feel so neglected. I have been away at conferences and church meetings most of the week and although tomorrow is my day off I am obligated to attend a meeting all afternoon, including supper, so I can't eat with the family.

Pastor Hashimoto brought a young lady in to see us on Saturday who is interested in becoming our new helper. She is just out of high school and doesn't speak English but she does seem to be capable of doing the work. She has a pleasant personality and seems to like working with children. This morning she told Lillian she could start next Wednesday. Lillian and I are worn out from trying to cope with our busy schedule and will certainly be glad to have some assistance.

Lillian seems to be beginning her third month of pregnancy. When I was in Tokyo, I talked to Dr. Syphers at the Seventh Day Adventist Hospital about Lillian's coming there for the birth of this Rh negative baby. He said he would be happy to care for her, but stressed the fact that we must realize the risk involved for "anything might happen."

Dr. Cary points out that in comparing hospitals we must realize that Dr. Syphers' has only two or three Rh negative cases a year whereas most U.S. hospitals have two or three a day. Ultimately the decision will probably depend on how fast Lillian's antibodies build up. Mary was born at Dr. Syphers' hospital and Lillian liked it. Housing before the birth would be a problem in Tokyo, but the trip to America would probably be a greater strain on Lillian and the baby than just going to Tokyo.

Lillian's weight is only 120 lbs. although she says she feels "very big around the waist." She has not been eating well, mainly soda crackers and pimento cheese, both expensive items here. Lillian guards them with her life. The other day I

couldn't resist trying one telling Lillian that after all I was
having a baby too! She also likes lemon flavoring in foods but
lemons are so expensive that she says she feels like a sinner
when she buys them. Oranges are quite reasonable. Tomatoes,
another item she likes, are expensive. We found a rare can of
stewed tomatoes in Kyoto the other day and splurged and got
it so we had a special treat for lunch today. We even bought
a couple of fresh tomatoes out of season this week to whet
Lillian's appetite.

Nov. 9, 1954

Doris Schneider will be taking over my work at Yao.
Sunday was my farewell and her welcome party after the
regular worship service. One high point of the celebration was
dressing us all in kimonos for a picture. Lillian said the *obi*
that women wear felt like a girdle and that it felt really good.
However the *zori* (thonged sandals) which are held on by a
thong between the big toe and the next toe were too tight and
hurt her feet so badly she could hardly keep them on long
enough for the picture.

Doris said the same thing about the *zori* they gave her to
wear. Most foreigners, who tend to have larger feet than the
Japanese, have the cord lengthened and then it is possible to
wear them with some degree of comfort. Lillian had to take a
milk break before we could finish the kimono pictures as she
said she felt like she was about to pass out.

After all the speeches and pictures Mrs. Yoshizawa (the
lady of the house where the church meets) served us a
delicious sukiyaki dinner. We got home about four and after
a short nap and a quick supper I went off to Kaizuka for the
evening worship there. Lillian went to bed soon after supper
and slept soundly until morning, exhausted by too much
activity and her pregnancy.

Monday we went to the Kobe area for a meeting with IBC
(interboard committee) missionaries. Mrs. Moran and Mrs.
Warner served hamburgers with all the trimmings, topped off
with apple pie and ice cream plus coffee. Lillian made it fine

until eight and then had to use an upstairs bed for a nap while the rest of us continued the meeting. It was good to meet Maurine Jones, Henry's wife. Originally they were supposed to go to India for industrial evangelism but couldn't get visas and so changed their plans and came to Japan.

I left early this morning for Wakayama and I expect to get home in time for supper tomorrow and then go to Nagoya early on Friday. The schedule is indeed hectic.

Takeda-san, who married Fujita-sensei one of our school teachers, has safely delivered a seven pound, eight ounce baby boy. With both parents having health problems we are grateful everything worked out so well. She sent word asking us to try to get her some baby diaper pins with plastic heads which she saw us using for Mary. Lillian is asking her mother to send them from America.

November 14, 1954

Last Thursday night Lillian got up to take care of Mary about 3 A.M. and then started shivering and feeling aches and pains all over. This continued all night, so the next day we called the doctor who got there in the early afternoon. The doctor diagnosed pneumonia and gave Lillian a shot of penicillin and some powdered medicine to take every four hours.

A shot of nutrients plus a second smaller shot of penicillin seemed to do the trick and Lillian's temperature fell from 103° to normal in three days. She has been ordered to stay in bed for a week, but the doctor is not coming back and has told her to stop taking medicine.

This seems to be about the middle of the third month of her pregnancy and, so far, there seems to be no ill effects on the baby. Dr. Cary continues to worry about the Rh negative factor and may order us home on that score.

Since I had to be away in Nagoya on Friday I was glad to have our new helper, Michiko Yamahara, with Lillian, plus our other capable Japanese friends who are always on call if they are needed.

Nov. 25, 1954

By Monday Lillian was able to go see Dr. Alice Cary in Kyoto. Since it is difficult for us to make the decision as to whether to stay here for the birth of the baby or go home, Dr. Cary made the decision for us. The risks for both Lillian and the baby are too great, she says, and we should go home on furlough. We have been here for four years now and the decision was made for us to go on regular furlough leaving Kobe January 18, 1955 on the *President Cleveland*—the same ship on which we came to Japan. We will get our train tickets from San Francisco to Baltimore through a travel agency in Japan and plan to arrive in Baltimore about February 5th, via Southern Pacific Railway.

Thursday was our annual United Church of Japan *(Kyodan)* missionary Thanksgiving dinner for this area. Some 32 of us, including 13 children, met at Alice Grube's home on the campus of Osaka Girl's School. For dinner there was a long table with place cards to indicate where we were to sit. For the first time Edward was seated with the children instead of with us, but Mary is still too little to be alone.

Liba Daub said our decision to go home was wise as she recently heard that of eight Rh babies born at the Tokyo hospital, four had died.

The dinner was like a family gathering and gave us a good opportunity to say farewell to our friends and co-workers. The turkeys were brought in by a caterer but everything else was home cooked. Each family brought two pies so about six we had pie and coffee again to fuel us for the trip back to our respective homes, after a wonderful day together.

Since it isn't a holiday here, I managed to excuse myself in the middle long enough to do our monthly shopping in Osaka while Lillian and the kids stayed with the group.

Edward is taking part in the Christmas program at the nursery and sternly informed us that he couldn't go to America before that. His suggestion is that Lillian and Michiko-san go to America and that he, Daddy and Mary stay here. He will miss his Japanese friends very much and we hope to find some new ones soon in Baltimore.

Lillian says it looks like the devil is out to get her but she hasn't given up yet! She said, "At Nojiri it was a constant battle with learning the language and ever since we returned it has been one thing after another: asthma, nausea, tiredness, pneumonia and now Mary has chicken pox!"

Fortunately, Edward already had chicken pox so we won't have to cope with two sick kids at once in the middle of a busy Christmas season. Lillian spends much of her time in bed and is afraid the cold weather will make her pneumonia flare up.

Dec. 5, 1954

Although Lillian is not able to take much part in them we are continuing the meetings in our home we had agreed to before Lillian got so sick. Friday the women of Nagano church were here for their Christmas celebration. I took over Lillian's duties as much as I could. She rested upstairs until 3 p.m. when the worship service was almost over and then was able to make a short talk about the need to love one another based on 1 John 4:7.

Several of the women are very antagonistic to one another and Lillian has been deeply concerned about this. At the end of the meeting I asked for sentence prayers after Lillian had gone back upstairs to rest. The first to pray was one who has caused most of the trouble and she prayed that they might remember the verse Lillian had given them and really love one another. She seemed most sincere and when I told Lillian she said, "I hope it wasn't just words." For refreshments we had pumpkin pie, coffee, nuts and candy. The children each had a present of a bag of candy.

Dec. 12, 1954

Last night Edward and I went to the annual Christmas dinner for all the various missionaries of this area. Lillian didn't feel up to it—the first one she has missed in four years. Mary stayed home with her so Edward and I brought home some of the Christmas goodies to share with them.

On Tuesday 16 Tondabayashi women came to see our Western-style house and visit with an American family. The group included the mayor's wife! By skipping a few of the formalities Lillian made it O.K. Michiko-san served everyone coffee and donuts.

Edward collided with his little friend Sat-chan and lost another tooth. Fortunately he doesn't let it bother him too much and shows with each smile what a toothless wonder he is. I tell him he needs to keep a few so he can enjoy all that good American food he will get on the ship home. He needs some encouragement to induce him to be willing to leave his many friends here. With our Tuesday open house bringing in new people almost every week he does not lack for friends.

Our annual Christmas form letter to friends and supporters features our friend, Pastor Toru Hashimoto this year. He heads up the rural center in Kawachi Nagano and is the pastor with whom we work most closely.

He underwent a period of severe Christian persecution in his childhood for his was the first family to become Christian in their small rural village in Hyogo Prefecture. As a result his family was "excommunicated" from their own relatives and from the village as a whole. A fine, equal to one week's wages, was imposed on anyone who dared to speak to them. They lived in a converted chicken house and were allowed only enough land to farm to make a meager living. Children threw stones at their house and no one visited them over a period of several years. Toru was ridiculed and laughed at by the children at school. Two members of another Christian family with less stability committed suicide under the pressure but Mr. Hashimoto and his family endured like the martyrs of the Early Church.

A Christian lawyer helped to vindicate them as falsely persecuted for their religion and Toru's father was later elected mayor of the village that had blackballed him. Pastor Hashimoto bears some psychological scars from this tragic experience, but he is amazingly free of bitterness and resentment toward his persecutors. He is 30, reads all the time, even standing on crowded trains—which is probably why he wears glasses. His wife is the daughter of a Baptist minister and they have two small children, Mitsuru-chan and Tomoko-chan.

He has helped to build up our Nagano church to more than double its original membership since coming here and has also provided inspiration and guidance in building our junior high school, kindergarten and nursery school. He helped start a new church in Tondabayashi, which now has its own pastor and church building, and has led the three churches of this area to unite as a cooperating "larger parish," called Kanan Mission. Each of these three churches gives their first Sunday offering to help start other new Sunday schools and churches in this area. He has also helped start many Sunday schools which meet in Christian homes in surrounding towns and villages.

With some scholarship help from the *Kyodan* (United Church), he is going to America next summer to study at Dubuque Seminary and Princeton Theological Seminary. He says that in the crisis of overwork and starting the new house church in Hatsushiba, he heard God speaking to him, like Christ spoke to Paul on the road to Damascus, saying, "I know you are exhausted, Toru, but keep up your good work for me and I will support you."

Our new helper, Michiko Yamahara, is not yet a Christian but she freely joins in our family worship and often takes part in the sentence prayers. She also attends church as often as she can. We expect her, along with a senior high girl from the local Buddhist school, to be baptized soon.

Dec. 20, 1954

A Christmas season is always a special opportunity to witness because many come to ask us what the celebration is all about. We usually have over 20 special Christmas celebrations in churches, homes and even factories. Yesterday I went to Kaizuka for an early Christmas celebration with about a thousand girls attending. After the meeting in the factory I

came back to Tomioka for a meeting, then in the afternoon to
Hatsushiba, returing to Kaizuka for an evening meeting. Four
meetings in three different towns is not unusual during the
Christmas season.

Last Tuesday we had 15 women attend our open house.
In addition Pastor Tokita, his wife and their baby girl, visited
with us most of the day and had dinner before leaving at
nine. We also had visits from another pastor and the young
girl from the Buddhist school who is entering a preparatory
class for baptism. Our open house tends to attract from two
or three visitors to as many as 25.

Dec. 27, 1954

Edward's nursery school Christmas program was a great
success with songs, skits and Bible stories about the meaning
of Christmas. Edward did his part well and Lillian gave a
greeting to the parents. She did well but cried for 15 minutes
after it was over. She was asked (as technical head of the
nursery) to explain why the nursery school had been forced
to move by the secular group. She didn't feel up to that so I
did it for her, which seemed to satisfy the parents.

Friday at nine, over one hundred carolers appeared for
refreshments and a closing worship service. Lillian, Michiko-
san and some volunteers from the Nagano women's association fed them cookies, nuts and cocoa. It was much easier this
year as we knew what to expect and were well prepared.

For Christmas Day dinner we had Pastor Hashimoto's
family, Shigeko-san and two bachelor ministers of the churches in Tomioka and Tondabayashi for turkey with all the
trimmings. I thought five-year-old Mitsura-chan would burst
from eating five times as much cranberry sauce as anyone else
did, but it didn't seem to hurt him. The Hashimotos stayed on
for supper and we played "Howdy-Doody" and "Western
Round-up." The children of the neighborhood all came in and
the older ones had a great time coloring and painting.

Jan. 2, 1955

New Year's Eve Lillian and I sat up until midnight playing checkers and popping corn in our fireplace. At midnight we welcomed the New Year in with a brief devotional service and retired. Japanese people usually go to bed early and get up at dawn on New Year's Day to spend the day, and several following it, in feasting, visiting, shooting firecrackers, visiting temples and shrines to pray for a good year. Some of them are too drunk with rice wine to know what they are doing.

Usually New Year's is the quietest time for us missionaries as the Japanese people are so busy with their own celebrations they seldom visit us. The children, however, are a different matter. Before breakfast Edward and Mary's friends were here eager to play. I spent the day flying kites, playing ball, popping corn and showing them colored slides of American scenes such as the national parks.

We had ham for a special treat for dinner that night.

Jan. 10. 1955

Our departure date has been changed to January 16. Although eight farewell meetings have been completed we still have visitors every day to say good-bye. Saturday my Japanese language teacher, Yagi-sensei, his wife and baby girl came for a sukiyaki farewell at noon. Just after they left two ministers appeared, so we brought out the sukiyaki and started all over again.

Lillian was worn out and went to bed while Michiko-san and I did the honors. The two ministers left before supper time but another fellow arrived and had supper with us. He is one of the evangelistic "caravaners" who travels with us each summer on our evangelistic tours of unchurched towns and villages.

On Sunday the Hayakawas came and stayed until two. I got back from Kaizuka in time to see them and then at four Debbie arrived and stayed and joined us for supper. Incidentally, our "caravaners" are planning to have another farewell shindig on the ship in the Kobe harbor just before we sail.

Farewell gifts have piled up so we had to send two extra boxes of things to the ship in Kobe—the most difficult being beautiful, but breakable, dolls in glass cases. The Japanese are probably the world's best givers of farewell parties and gifts. We have been advised to take an extra suitcase along to the ship as there are sure to be a few people coming to see us off with last minute gifts in hand. Fortunately we will be on a ship and not on an airplane.

Jan. 18, 1955—aboard the SS President Cleveland *at Yokohama*

The trip to the ship in Kobe Harbor was easier than we expected because Mack Warner, a missionary friend, kindly transported us there in his roomy station wagon. The rest of Saturday was a blur showing guests around the ship, getting settled in our cabin and wiping away tears when friends sang "God Be With You" as we pulled out of the harbor.

Yesterday, Sunday, we attended Union Church in Tokyo while the ship lay at anchor and met many missionary friends from our Lake Nojiri vacation days. Only missionary friends welcomed us to Japan on arrival four years ago, but now even a Japanese newspaper joined in the farewell festivities, telling of our work in Japan and printing a not-too-flattering picture of me to illustrate it.

The ship food is fantastic.

Sequel

We lost the Rh baby in spite of returning to one of the best equipped hospitals in the U.S. There is a mystery beyond our understanding.

Yet we could not let this tragedy avert us from continuing our service to the people in Japan. On April, 23, 1956 we arrived back in Japan, via Yokohama, and continued to serve there for more than 20 years.

Following our return we completed the development of three churches where I was the organizing pastor and helped in the formation of six more new churches. We continued to serve on the board of directors of two Christian schools: Osaka Jo Gakuin in Osaka and Seikyo Gakuen in Kawachinagano. In addition to our church-development work, we continued some part-time teaching.

Much of the development of Seikyo Gakuen Christian School is recorded in the photo section of this book. Although the school began with a kindergarten program in 1934, the Seikyo Gakuen name was not used until the beginning of the junior high program in 1951. Starting with 40 students, the high school program had grown to over 2,000 students in 1992. Now they have bought land for a college program which they hope to start in the next couple years. Osaka Jo Gakuin has already developed a junior college program that is quite successful.

Although now retired, I keep my membership on Seikyo Gakuen's Board of Directors because of their insistence. We correspond regularly and Lillian and I participated in the 50th anniversary celebration of the kindergarten in 1984.

We look forward with hope to being able to participate in the opening ceremonies for the college program, which we trust will not be long delayed. Four schools in Japan, including one non-Christian school, are using my book, *Mission Adventures In Many Lands,* as a supplementary reader for English classes. May God use it to lead many Japanese young people to faith in Jesus Christ.

We constantly thank God who enabled us to learn the language and culture of Japan well enough to serve there. Our hopes and dreams for the continuing development of Christianity in Japan are summarized in the following postscript.

Postscript

Christianity's Challenge to Japan

The Japanese Christian novelist, Shusaku Endo, says that for him accepting Christianity was like putting on an ill-fitting foreign suit of clothes. He indicates that he feels very uncomfortable in this "foreign" suit of clothes. However, he also implies that he would be even more uncomfortable if he were not wearing that strange suit. After all, he does not want to be left spiritually naked, and Christianity is the best-fitting religion he can find.

Significantly, the popularity of Christian novels by prizewinning authors, such as Shusaku Endo and Ayako Miura, testify to Japan's interest in Christianity. As a missionary who has served more than 20 years in Japan, I think Endo's analogy could be applied to the nation of Japan, as well as to him individually.

Japan is far from accepting this "foreign suit of religious clothing" en masse, but many Japanese people are making some attempts to see how well the Christian faith might fit—now or in the future.

A recent survey by the Roman Catholic church discovered that 33% of the Japanese had attended church at sometime; over 30% of the homes in big cities like Tokyo and Osaka have Bibles; and 43% of young people under 30 have their own Bible. The Bible is a best seller in Japan and in 1989 700,000 Bibles were purchased. The so-called "evangelicals" claim they have distributed or sold over 5,500,000 Bibles in their new version, the *New Japanese Bible*. Christian radio and television programs are available to 95% of Japan's population and some 100 theological schools offer Christian training to an estimated 3,000 students.

This all in strong contradiction to statistics that say only one percent of Japanese people are committed Christians.

Japan's *Asahi* newspaper made a religious survey in 1981 which maintained that 27% of the people said they were Buddhist; 4% said they were Shinto; and 2% said they were Christian. Amazingly, this survey indicated that 62% said they had no formal membership in any religion.

What does this mean? Could it be that the Japanese are in an "in-between" stage—where they are beginning to leave the traditional religions but are not yet ready to accept the "ill-fitting" Christian religion? Sitting on the fence is an uncomfortable position. As this becomes increasingly uncomfortable, will the Christian suit become more fitting than sitting on the fence? Or, will they prefer the ill-fitting Christian suit rather than remain spiritually unclothed?

People usually turn to religion in times of poverty, disease or war. But one NHK news commentator says that as Japan becomes disillusioned with the shallowness of ambition and affluence, this may drive them to seek truth on a deeper level.

Christianity made a strong beginning in Japan when the Spanish Jesuit priest, Father Francis Xavier, first brought Christianity there in 1549. Some think that this Christian beginning in Japan failed because it was rejected by the populace. The opposite is true. It was crushed because so many of the people accepted Christianity the ruling shoguns of Japan feared Christianity would take over the country religiously and politically.

What the political danger was of Spain or Portugal taking over Japan at that time remains unclear. However, it is certain that the Shogun Hideyoshi, and those who followed him, perceived such domination as a real danger. To protect themselves from this threat, they finally banished Christianity completely—and closed Japan's doors to the outside world for over 200 years.

Some reports indicate that there were a thousand churches or preaching places in Japan at the time of the expulsion. Over 30,000 Christians are reported to have been massacred by the ruling shogunate in 1638 where, being persecuted, they had joined a rebellion by followers of several Christian feudal lords whose retainers made a final stand at Shimabara.

If it is true that "the blood of the martyrs is the seed of the church," then Japan certainly deserves to have a strong Christian church, now or in the future.

While no clear records are available, it would appear more Christians were martyred in Japan than in Rome. With such a sacrifice, it would seem that just as Rome became the leader for Christianity in the West, Japan is poised to become the leader of Christianity in the East.

Even accepting the figure of only 2% of the population being Christians in Japan, the leadership figures are larger, for the percentage of Christian delegates elected to the upper and lower house of the Diet has ranged from some 3% to 5%. Surely this would indicate the leadership potential in this country for Christianity in the future.

During World War II Japan showed its military might. Today it is showing its economic strength. Perhaps in the future Japan will demonstrate its power in the religious realm.

What would it take for Japan to become a strong Christian nation? It already has a work ethic similar to the "Protestant work ethic" of America. But other ingredients are necessary.

Surely needed is the development of more upstanding Christian leaders such as Kanzo Uchimura (a great Bible teacher and publisher of Christian study materials) and Toyohiko Kagawa (who was unique in his ability to keep the two basic Christian elements of social action and evangelism together in one effective Christian approach to people. Like his Lord, Jesus Christ, Kagawa showed his concern for the needs of the whole person: physical needs, mental needs and spiritual needs).

These leadership patterns need to be duplicated many

times over. And this leadership development must include women like the effective educator, Michi Kawai, and the former head of Japan's YWCA, Rev. Mrs. Uemura (who was ordained by the Japan church before most American churches began to ordain women).

Another necessary ingredient is the development of a style and form of Christianity which is more indigenous to Japan. The church in Japan has too slavishly followed the Western model in church architecture and in the form of worship. To make Christianity more acceptable to Japanese worshippers, why not use Japanese musical instruments such as the *koto* and *shamisen* in worship service? Why not develop church buildings that fit in more naturally with Japanese religious ideas—churches that follow the graceful lines of a Buddhist temple for example.

A third need for Christian advance is to make a greater effort to respect Japan's close family ties and sense of group unity. Why not try harder to convert whole families, rather than just one individual who becomes isolated from the family? In Japan people making individual decisions may be charged with disloyalty to the group. A popular proverb says, "The nail that sticks out will get hammered down." Sometimes that happens to a Christian who makes an individual decision to join the church. That's why we need to try harder to convert families, not just individuals.

Regarding the problem of church buildings, we might learn something from a new religious group which developed out of Nichiren Buddhism. Deciding it would grow faster if it held meetings in the homes of its members and not build expensive buildings, this group, Soka Gakkai, grew rapidly. Their political arm is the second or third strongest group in the government. They train lay leaders to advance their work and reward them well. If this pattern works well in Japan, why not make use of it?

One branch of Christianity in Japan which has tried this home meeting approach in the past is the group called "churchless Christianity" (*Mukyokai*), started by the above-mentioned Kanzo Uchimura. It is based on Bible study in private homes and depends on lay leadership without the use of an ordained clergy. One of the presidents of Japan's prestigious University of Tokyo came from this "churchless Christianity" group.

Perhaps by following such a pattern, we could expect more rapid Christian growth in expensive Japan.

Much preparing of the Japanese soil for Christianity has been done. Father Francis Xavier began it in 1549. There was a long break when Japan was closed to the outside world for two centuries and Christians were branded as "disloyal" to Japan's religious and political traditions.

When Japan reopened its doors in 1859 many denominations entered the country and began preparing the soil again—through evangelism, building churches and starting Christian schools.

Hundreds of thousands of Japanese students have graduated from schools begun by Christians. For many of them this is the first step toward becoming a Christian. There are now over 7,000 churches and preaching places all over Japan which include the mainline denominations, the so-called "evangelicals" and the churches started by independent mission boards and para-church groups.

Showing considerable inner strength and vigor the church in Japan has sent out over 300 missionaries to 36 other lands, especially to Latin American countries where Japanese immigrants live.

For two centuries Christianity was persecuted in Japan, but now with the emperor married to a graduate of a Christian school, we are past that tragic stage.

It would appear that Japan is ready for a major Christian advance. If the church of Jesus Christ is faithful in preparing the soil and planting the gospel seed, God may surprise us with a great harvest in that beautiful country.

Is Japan likely to become a strong Christian land in the immediate future? Maybe not. However, knowing the ability of the small church that exists there plus the Japanese potential for creative leadership and growth, it would seem we could justifiably be optimistic about the future.

It is quite possible that Japan may, someday, become the Christian leader for all the Far East. If the thriving church in Korea should surpass Japan in this leadership role, then more power to Korea. Better yet, what if these two traditional enemies joined forces—the promising Japanese church and the thriving Korean church—to become joint leaders in the development of Christianity in Asia?

Index

Ainu, 138

Alien Registration Cards, 17, 131

Baptism, 43-44, 67, 77, 132, 160

Bathing practices, 6-7, 31, 51, 78, 85, 86

Bedding (*futon*), 5, 35, 40, 51, 73

Biwa, Lake, 17

Bowing, 69, 139

Buddhism 13, 16, 34, 41, 56, 82, 105

Bunraku puppets, 73, 103

Buraku-bito (Eta, "outcast"), 53, 121, 131

Brunner, Emil, 145

Earthquakes, 59, 104, 107

Emperor: calendar by reign, 75; palaces, 6; reverence for, 10, 29, 116, 122; new, 169

Fertilizer (human waste) 30, 104

Festivals and holidays: *Aki Matsuri* (Fall Festival), 34; Children's Day, 12, 140; Christmas, 13, 42-44, 46, 72-73, 109, 113-116, 127, 147, 156-160; Constitution Day, 122; Culture Day, 69; Doll

Festival, 12; Emperor's Birthday, 122; Founding of the Nation Day, 122, New Year's, 13, 43, 72, 75, 114-117, 160-161; O-bon, 13; *Tanabata* (Vega), 13

Fuchida, Capt. Mitsuo, 41, 129-130

Fuji, Mt., 19-21

Funerals, 49, 106, 118, 141

Gift giving, 12, 34, 39, 51, 58, 69, 71, 85, 106, 114, 117, 143, 161

Hashimoto, Toru, 10, 25, 35-36, 44-45, 49, 51-54, 66-67, 72, 74, 79, 88, 90-91, 101, 106, 109, 111, 115, 125, 132-134, 143, 147-148, 150-151, 153, 158, 160

Hiroshima, 70

Illness: anemia, 50, 60, 62, 65; asthma, 70, 108-109, 157; boils, 105, 147; chicken pox, 45, 157; diphtheria, 111; dysentery, 18; measles, 8, 137; peritonitis, 50-51, 68, 73, 141; pneumonia, 155, 157; trachoma, 31, 86; tuberculosis, 49

Larry and Lillian Driskill here share wisdom gleaned from serving as missionaries to Japan for over 20 years. Those planning to live or work in a different culture or those planning to travel abroad will find their cross-cultural insights fascinating and practical. This informative book chronicles how the Driskills learned to adjust to another culture and thus is especially valuable in preparing new missionaries or business people to live and serve in other lands. It also documents what is required of those who would love and serve God's people in different lands.